BECOMING

BECOMING _____

(insert your name here)

ANNA SYMONDS

BECOMING YOU BECOMING

_____

(insert your name here)

Matador
9 De Montfort Mews
Leicester LE1 7FW, UK
Tel: (+44) 116 255 9311 / 9312
Email: books@troubador.co.uk
Web: www.troubador.co.uk/matador

ISBN 978-1906221-775

Typeset in 12pt Bembo by Troubador Publishing Ltd, Leicester, UK
Printewd in the UK by The Cromwell Press Ltd, Trowbridge, Wilts

Matador is an imprint of Troubador Publishing Ltd

FOR

Rachael Crawley
(insert your name here)

This book has been written for you.

Contents

Introduction

Me, Myself And I

A few days after I started at secondary school, our class had to vote for a form captain. We wrote down the name of the person we thought would be suitable. And it turned out that I was the choice! (Before you imagine that I was always the kind of girl who got chosen for things, I can truly say that I absolutely was not).

I remember being completely shocked. I couldn't think of a single thing that would have made anyone notice me. I wasn't classed as *particularly* pretty, I wasn't *especially* popular, I didn't have any obvious *exceptional* talent. A handful of people loved me and thought I was special. But in the eyes of the big wide world, as far as I knew, there was nothing that marked me out. I thought of myself as a very ordinary girl.

One girl even told me she was pleased I'd been chosen because I was 'so normal'. She obviously saw 'normal' as a good thing, desirable even. But although it was better than her thinking I was some kind of weird freak, I didn't find it wonderfully flattering.

Deep down I didn't want to be ordinary. I wanted to be exceptional! I wanted to be significant and I wanted my life to matter.

We're in this together...

Circumstances, age, nationality and experiences may separate us. But from the woman wrapped up in newspaper huddled in a shop doorway, to the one who moves in a private jet between her luxury homes, wherever we live, and whatever our title, the status and address of you, me and everybody else is actually the same:

Temporary Resident
Planet Earth

The number of years we spend here varies but no woman is given unlimited time. And buried somewhere inside us, like in the 10 year old me, hides a desire to find a way to make our stay count for something, to feel that there's been some point in us being alive.

We don't want to be plain 'ordinary' women. But unsure of ourselves and where we're going, we've allowed our identity to be defined by what others think and say about us; what we can do, have and achieve; and in our past and present relationships. We've become labelled over the years and got further away from who we really are and our dreams of who we could be.

'JUST BE YOURSELF' could be the title of so many films and novels. Their heroine faces a variety of challenges that teach her that the way to be happy, and for people to like and respect her, is to lose some of the props she's relied on to create her identity and just be the woman she really is. Like that she's far more interesting and fulfilled than as any of the other women she tried to be.

"Just be yourself" is favourite advice of counsellors, agony aunts, relationship experts, parents and friends. Somehow we know it's good advice too but actually following it isn't as straightforward as it looks in the pages of a book or on the big screen. You aren't alone if you don't really know who you are — apart from your job description, the role you fulfil in your home or the school you once went to — or how to find out.

Mostly we don't know where to begin to discover who we are and what's more, we're not sure we want to. We doubt that we'd unearth anything worth finding. And we don't necessarily want to be ourselves anyway — we don't suppose we'd be admired for it. We may dream, if we allow ourselves to dream at all, of being beautiful, confident, popular, fulfilled women but we can't imagine becoming like that if we 'just be yourself'.

...but there's only one of each of us...

200 of your cells could fit on this full stop → . ←. And each one of those miniscule cells carries your unique DNA. Your identity is etched on every single tiniest part of your body – your iris could serve as your ID card and so could your fingerprints.

...and YOU are no 'ordinary' woman!

We know we're unique and don't pay very much attention to it. But if you do pause for a moment and give it some thought, you begin to see that it is actually completely mind blowing. Of all the zillions of people who have ever lived, and will ever live, not one could be mistaken for you. You have a unique personality, a unique mind and a unique potential to bring a unique style and creativity to *everything* you put your hand to. As an original, there must be some things for you to express that no one else can.

You may believe you just happened – by some accident of the universe – but what a happening! Have you ever stopped to wonder that if your design is so precise, then surely it must mean that great care and intent went into it? Or have you looked to find your place in the world without considering that – without much thought for whoever made this beautiful Earth your address?

Few of us have given any consideration to the someone who made us unique. We haven't paused to see that to 'just be yourself' implies that someone somewhere must have made a self for us to be. We haven't considered that if they went to all that trouble then perhaps it was with some purpose in mind – perhaps the answer to the question of our identity lies with them. We haven't asked what it could mean if that someone was God.

Becoming You

I believe that you were made by God, designed with so much care and intent. I believe that He had a plan when He made you unique, personalised your DNA, made you a woman, breathed life into you and put you on Planet Earth. And I believe that you can discover His plan and find fulfilment when you live it.

Whatever circumstances and stage of life you find yourself in today:

- It is never too late or too difficult, whatever you have gone through in your life, however many times you have failed at things, or however ancient you feel, to become the person you were designed to be. Yes, *designed* to be!

- You are worth it. Whatever you may believe about your lack of value, you are worthy of discovering and becoming the woman God envisaged when He envisaged you. And you will not be disappointed by the treasure and potential you find within yourself.

- It is worth it. How do I know? I have experienced highs and lows. I have felt as if I have been to the ends of the earth to find some point for being alive. But all any of that has shown me is that no one and nothing, not one single earthly thing – not even me myself – can give my life lasting meaning.

  It was only in turning to God that I began to see that He had created me with worthwhile and significant purpose and He alone could show me how to become the woman I had been designed to be, and to live the life that had been waiting for me to live.

- So it can actually happen!
  Whether you believe in God – or not, if you don't know the wonder and truth of who you really are, and of all you've been created to achieve, then:

This Book Is For YOU

This book has been written to tell you how to go about **BECOMING** _____. It's easy to follow. You can use it at your
(insert your name here)
own speed and in your own way. It doesn't just paint lots of lovely pictures of what life could look like; it takes you step by step through how to get there.

This really can be your opportunity to find out who you've been designed to be and how to gain the confidence to be that woman, living in the fullnesss of your created purpose.

You have nothing to lose and everything to gain! So grab a pen, write your name into the title and make this world wait no longer for the emergence of the unique and amazing woman you truly are!

BEFORE

I

The Woman You See

Welcome to **BECOMING** ___*Rachael*___! It's part
(insert your name here)
book, part workbook, so as you read these pages, you'll write yourself into
them. And as you do, you'll be stunned and thrilled to discover the truth
about who you really are and what you're purposed for – the unique and
wonderful potential in you to make a difference, and be amazing, on the
Earth.

That Woman You See

Although you may not realise it, you carry a picture of yourself around in
your imagination. It's probably not a detailed, photo-quality image but an
impression of who and what you think you really are. So what is your image
of yourself like? Try focusing in on it to see. Close your eyes, imagine
yourself in a crowded room full of glamorous strangers and zoom in for a
closer look:

What are you doing?

Laughing and joking. Being silly.

What do your eyes look like?

Blue. No glasses? Crinkled from laughing but also annoyed at annoying people.

What's the expression on your face?

Laughter. Mouth open, teeth on show. Eyes wideish, crinkled.

What are you wearing?

My Primark dress thing & leggings. My hair is blonder.

What posture do you have?

Stood up, bent slightly back because i'm laughing at someone/something.

Are you looking at a confident, relaxed woman, who is free and at ease, or an anxious, awkward, tense person, nervously dominating conversation or conscious of wanting to defend herself and hide?

Confident, pretty relaxed, bit tense, fairly free but still trapped.

Yourself And You

When you were considering the way you see yourself, did you notice that you had an opinion about that woman you could see? Do you realise that you actually have a relationship with yourself?

Imagine YOU were going to tell YOURSELF – that woman you focused in on just now – what YOU think of her. What are your feelings towards her? There are some words below to help with this. Circle any that stand out or write down your own:

~~critical of her~~	judgmental of her	~~frustrated by her~~
annoyed with her	dislike towards her	hate towards her
~~love for her~~	tenderness towards her	sympathy for her
pity for her	wanting to give her a hug	that she's ugly
that she's stupid	that she's beautiful	that she's a failure

And how does YOURSELF – that woman you focused in on – feel when she sees YOU approaching to tell her what YOU think of her?

scared	ashamed	embarrassed	~~optimistic~~
full of dread	~~confident~~	rebellious	~~pleased to see you~~

So who is this woman you see?

Having considered the way you think of yourself, in your view:

Would you call yourself beautiful?

Yes. God made me and I'm normally comfortable, happy even, with how I look.

Would you say you are lovable – do you/ can you love yourself?

Yes. Of course I can love myself, God calls me too. But sometimes I want to be someone else.

Do you think you matter? In your opinion, do you have a significant and worthwhile purpose for being alive?

Yes. But I don't know what my purpose is and that can be frustrating. Sometimes I feel stuck in a rut, like there's no point to anything.

Shame

You should have a clearer idea of the way you see yourself. Did your feelings surprise you in any way? *who I want to be.*

*I found it hard to picture me as I am, I normally picture**

If anyone had asked me a few years ago if I liked myself, I would have said I did. But one day I considered my relationship with myself in more detail and I realised that I actually despised myself for being less than good enough, on the one hand, and felt threatened by my own negative judgments on the other.

It was as if I could see that my whole life had been about the missing percent. That I was never endingly lacking in some way. I realised that I was always waiting for the 'BUT': "I love you, BUT…" "That was good, BUT…". Not everyone had treated me that way in reality. It was something deep inside me that made me feel I couldn't relax in anyone's affection, including my own, because I knew there was always something about myself that could be improved.

There's an awareness deep in the heart of humankind that we're not all we could be. We live in SHAME:

A PAINFUL EMOTION RESULTING FROM AN
AWARENESS OF HAVING DONE SOMETHING
DISHONOURABLE, UNWORTHY OR FOOLISH.
Collins Dictionary

THE PAINFUL EMOTION ARISING FROM THE
CONSCIOUSNESS OF SOMETHING DISHONOURING,
RIDICULOUS, OR INDECOROUS IN ONE'S OWN
CONDUCT OR CIRCUMSTANCES.
Oxford English Dictionary

Why do we have shame?

To find out why we have shame, we need to go right back to the beginning
of time. It takes quite a leap of the imagination to envisage life for Adam
and Eve in the garden of Eden, reigning over the world, enjoying
relationships with God and each other in this perfectly beautiful place.
Nothing horrible or jarring. Just peace, beauty and happiness:

> *Although Adam and his wife were both naked, neither of them felt any*
> **shame.**
> (Genesis 2:25 NLT)

Just think of it. They felt relaxed, completely at ease, comfortable,
unthreatened, confident, happy, attractive, free and uninhibited.

And then devastation. And how completely traumatic and horrific it must
have seemed. The devil lured Eve to do the one thing God had told her not
to: to eat the forbidden fruit. And from that moment, sin had entered the
perfect world and brought destruction and shame in its wake:

> *Their eyes were opened, and they suddenly felt* **shame** *at their*
> *nakedness.*
> (Genesis 3:7 NLT)

They must have felt so self-conscious, anxious, awkward, tense, inferior,
inhibited and undesirable.

What does shame do to us?

All the ease Adam and Eve felt had gone. They hid in their shame, afraid. Afraid of being seen, of being found out, of being rejected:

> *They strung fig leaves together around their hips to cover themselves.*
> *Toward evening they heard the Lord God walking about in the garden, so*
> *they* **hid themselves** *among the trees.*
> (Genesis 3:7-8 NLT)

Sin entered the world through Adam and Eve and we are all born corrupted by its poison – spiritually, morally and physically. We have dark capacities and they show very quickly. As we grow up, we don't feel beautiful. We feel wrong about ourselves, that there's something amiss somewhere. We've inherited an inferiority complex, a sense of shame and unworthiness that dominates us. Like for Adam and Eve, our shame causes us to fear being exposed.

Feeling uncomfortable about ourselves, we're uncertain of our identity and we measure our value by how acceptable, desirable and successful we are compared with other people. We want who we are to be appreciated and what we do to be admired but other people's reactions to us tend to confirm our worst fears that we're not good enough. Even if some people have shown us genuine love and acceptance, there will have been others who haven't.

In pursuit of acceptance, we hide and reinvent ourselves. We're deeply affected by the impact we have on other people. If we're praised for things, even things we didn't like doing, or think we were very accomplished at, we'll often continue doing those things to keep the positive attention. And we may copy things that seem to make other people desirable. In the process, we find that we've lost sight

Have your feelings of shame been intensified by rejection, criticism, failure, abuse, abandonment, being teased and laughed at or just by going unnoticed – never really seeming to matter? Even if you receive love and affirmation, do you retain a nagging feeling of not being all you could be?

of who we really are, and what we want, and our lives can become a mixture of hiding and performing.

Look at the picture *"I Feel Ugly"* on the next page. It shows what happens when our lives are rooted in shame.

"I FEEL UGLY"

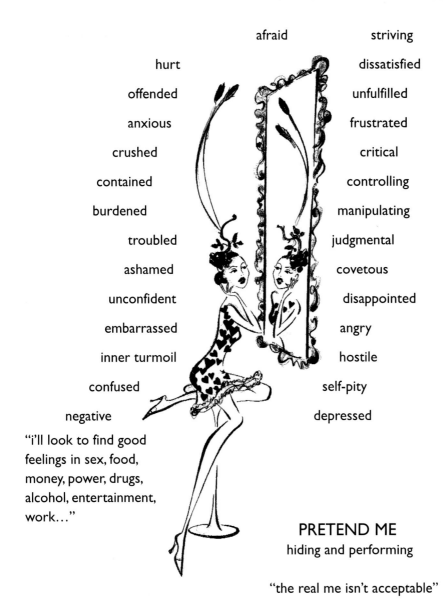

afraid
striving

hurt
dissatisfied

offended
unfulfilled

anxious
frustrated

crushed
critical

contained
controlling

burdened
manipulating

troubled
judgmental

ashamed
covetous

unconfident
disappointed

embarrassed
angry

inner turmoil
hostile

confused
self-pity

negative
depressed

"i'll look to find good feelings in sex, food, money, power, drugs, alcohol, entertainment, work…"

PRETEND ME
hiding and performing

"the real me isn't acceptable"

"something's wrong with me"

SHAME   GUILT   ABUSE   REJECTION

2

The Woman You See
In The Mirror

Do you find that the way you see yourself is affected by the way you feel about your body and appearance?

Yes.

The Stats

98% of women are unhappy with their bodies.[1]
70% believe their bodies stop them having the life they want.[2]
42% are jealous of good looking women friends.[2]
58% are jealous of women their age who look younger. [2]
36% envy all younger women.[2]
50% think climbing the career ladder would be easier if they were better looking.[2]
8/10 feel celebrity culture has distorted men's perceptions of them.[2]
If they had a better body, 12% would change partner.[2]

A Woman's Shame

Rather than realising that we need to find a way of fixing the shame that is the result of the fall, we get the idea that we'd feel right and good about ourselves if we could only become popular and successful. **And for women this seems to depend on**

> **Do you relate to feelings of dissatisfaction and striving for beauty, popularity and success to get rid of feeling ugly, stupid, awful, ridiculous, horrible, disgusting, frumpy, a failure...?** *Yes.*

our appearance: that being admired for who we are and what we do relies on how we look.

Adverts for things like skin cream, makeup and clothes seem to be pictures of what would happen if we could get rid of the shame. If we were perfect, truly fabulous, then wouldn't we be LOVED? Wouldn't we WOW the world?

That's what happens to Cinderella. She gets a dazzling makeover on her appearance and it is as if the shame is gone. This inferior, abused nobody becomes desirable and finds true love, wealth, status, a palace to call home and a happy ever after ending!

Although physical perfection is undefined, we have a strong sense that we fail to measure up to it. Our concept of the ideal appearance depends on our conditioning. The culture and times we live in affect what's being aspired to. In 21st century Britain, that's youthful; slender and toned; a flawless, possibly tanned, at least healthily glowing complexion and the 'right', fashionable and probably expensive clothes and accessories.

> **VOICE OF SHAME**
> *"Feeling stupid, disgusting and a failure makes me ambitious and obsessed with my body and clothes because if I could become successful and beautiful, finally I wouldn't be inferior. I'd have superiority. And if I was better than everyone else, then wouldn't I be shameless?"*

> **VOICE OF SHAME**
> *"Shame seems to be all the bad things I feel about myself: ugly, unacceptable, unlovable, unworthwhile, valueless."*

It is measuring ourselves against that idea of perfection that controls what we think when we look in the mirror. We have a tendency to see ourselves in bits and not as a whole. We see fat ankles; completely miss the lovely legs, body and face they're attached to; feel unhappy and as if we are entirely unattractive; and then we hate ourselves.

We see and hear so many things in the mirror: the girls' laughter, your mother's criticism, an unflattering nickname, being rejected for your lack of sex appeal or wanted for nothing else, envious sneering, all the times no one noticed you, the things you overheard, the motivation behind the compliments.

They either leave us defeated so we give up on our appearance altogether. Or they spur us on to try ever harder to look better.

> **Average British woman worries about the size and shape of her body every 15 minutes. About 1/3 of women worry about their body 'every waking minute'.[1]**

Magazines come under a lot of criticism for promoting a message that success and happiness mean being impossibly beautiful, stylish and thin. But is it fair?

> **70% of women feel DEPRESSED, GUILTY and SHAMEFUL after 3 minutes looking at a fashion magazine.[2]**

There is certainly a lot of distortion in the magazines' pages as they cleverly manipulate images to present a standard that is largely unobtainable.

Makeup artist Charlotte Tilbury describes one method of deception: "To smooth models' faces and to make their eyes more feline, I use a gadget with cosmetic sticky tape and a band — the tape attaches to the skin at the temples then the band is secured behind the head in the hair."[4] (You can see the process of preparing a model for a

> **The average US woman: 5 foot 3 inches, 152 pounds. The average model: 5 foot 9 inches, 110 pounds.[3]**

> VOICE OF SHAME
>
> *"I realise I feel so ugly and horrible — actually REPULSIVE and I always have — as if I DISGUST people. It's why I try to use clothes to stop offending people's eyes and beings so much. I was so aware of this going into that room, that the space all around me would make people feel repelled. That's a horrible feeling. I feel hated, rejected, mocked, loathed by the world. In my family, at church, at any event, at school — actually everywhere — all my life. As if people are allergic to me, that I'd better just hide away so I don't offend."*

magazine shoot at www.campaignforrealbeauty.com).

These images the magazines present do contribute to women's insecurities – most women bring magazines up as a significant factor in making them feel unhappy with themselves. But we've got to ask ourselves: Aren't the magazines appealing to the shame that's already in women? Don't they just **CONFIRM** the sense that success and happiness are indeed derived from being beautiful, stylish and thin? Don't they reflect us before they define us? Don't we have to face the fact that the problem begins in being fallen?

They present celebrities for us to model ourselves on because we demand people we can emulate, whose style we can copy in the hope that it will make us more desirable. But we find out that they are held together by their stylists, diet coaches and fitness trainers. They too are looking for the elusive something that will help them to relax in their skin.

Body Image Quiz

Try this quiz and see how shame is affecting the way you feel about your body:

1. How have you felt about your appearance throughout your life? Mark crosses on the lines to correspond with how happy or unhappy you felt in each of the relevant age ranges. Think about why you felt the way you did or why your feelings changed. If anything comes to mind, note it down.

Under 10

UNHAPPY ——————————————— X ——— HAPPY

WHY?

I was never "the popular one" and guys never desired me (in the way primary school is) that much... Some did. But I was blissfully unaware of image problems.

11-14

UNHAPPY ———— X ———————————————— HAPPY

WHY?

I changed myself to stop being bullied but there was still a part of me that was unaware of image issues.

15-20

UNHAPPY X ————————————→ X ——— HAPPY

WHY?

I went from anorexic at 17 to now at 19 being fairly comfortable in my own skin. I haven't been wearing makeup lately but I often look for ways to "improve myself" / identity issues.

20's

UNHAPPY ——————————————————— HAPPY

WHY?

30's
UNHAPPY _____ HAPPY
WHY?

40's
UNHAPPY _____ HAPPY
WHY?

50's
UNHAPPY _____ HAPPY
WHY?

60's
UNHAPPY _____ HAPPY
WHY?

70's
UNHAPPY _____ HAPPY
WHY?

80's and above
UNHAPPY _____ HAPPY
WHY?

2. There are possibly parts of your body you like and parts you don't like. Think about what they are and why you feel the way you do. What has shaped your view about the ideal way to look?

I like:	Because:
My hair.	It's been professionally straightened so it never goes frizzy and I get many more compliments.
My waist.	It creates a Audrey Hepburn style hourglass figure.
My tummy. (most of the time)	It's pretty flat.
My boobs (half thalf?)	I like the shape they give me.
My eyes.	Big blue eyes. My lips: full!!

I dislike:	Because:
My legs.	They're short and stumpy and covered with cellulite
My boobs:	too big!
My tummy:	could be smaller & flatter!
My arms:	big & flabby.
My hair (at times):	too flat.
My stretchmarks:	ew! I can't wear shorts!

I want to be/have:	Because:
Long, slim legs with no cellulite.	That's what models have and what men like.
& no stretch marks!	I can wear shorts confidently!
Smaller boobs:	more clothing options & my waist would be more visible.
Toned	: model look
Longer, thicker hair:	more possibilities & looks healthier.
Perkier bum:	Kim Kardashian!!

3. How do your feelings about yourself affect your life? How do you think your life would change if you had your ideal appearance you described above? Would you have more time/ spend less money/ be happier/ feel freer/ have your life controlled less by worries about your weight and what to eat/ do things you're prevented from at the moment because of the way you look?

They don't affect me too much, just at times I get consumed by thoughts of the "new me". My life wouldn't change that much but I'd feel like people would relate to me better, I'd be more feminine & guys would desire me (not always a good thing!) I'd possibly feel happier but realistically not, maybe be freer, less consumed. I could wear shorts!!

4. Go to any magazine stand and you'll see certain magazines are filled with criticism of the way celebrities look. They draw attention to lipstick marks on their teeth, stretch marks, rolls of flab, wrinkles, cosmetic surgery scars, 'frumpy' outfits etc. One of the magazines even draws a red circle around the offending flaw, calling it the 'circle of shame'. Are you scared of criticism of your appearance, paranoid even about being embarrassed and humiliated?

Not really, but I would be mortified if it happened. I don't mind chatting with my girl mates about my flaws. Hey, I'm a woman of God; human! But if a guy pointed them out or someone I looked upto / respected did, I'd be horrified & upset.

5. How do you react to other women? Do you compare
    yourself against them? Are you critical? Judgmental?
    Resentful? Competitive? Fearful? Do you find yourself
    feeling envious and covetous of how they look and the clothes
    they have? Or like the magazines do, do you enjoy criticising
    other women, feeling smug and relieved when you notice
    'flaws' in them?

    Quite often I find myself looking for
    myself in them. I do sometimes compare
    myself. I pick up on good hair/makeup/
    thinner than me & that "inspires" me to
    try harder. I try not to be judgemental/
    critical but i can be. I feel like women
    don't find me feminine so struggle to relate to me

6. How much are you affected by wondering/worrying what
    men feel about you?

    Not too much. I do catch myself
    slotting people into "leagues" & at times
    think I'm below someone's league or
    I'm above someone elses. I do want to
    be desired & seen as beautiful, but I
    feel like I'm seen as the silly kid sister.

7. Would you say you feel free to develop your own personal
    style or would you fear being judged for it and tend more
    towards copying other people?

    I feel pretty free but sometimes I hang
    back eg wearing red lipstick for no
    reason to uni = people picking up &
    maybe making fun.

8. Do you have your own set of clothes rules you follow – things
    that you won't/must wear for whatever reasons? Where do
    you think these limitations have come from?

    *Not really but I'm starting to. I'm trying to
    dress more for my shape so my clothes
    are more flattering perhaps.*

9. Do you use your clothes or makeup, or wish you knew how,
    to conceal or correct yourself or to make up for the lack you
    feel in yourself, to make you more desirable or acceptable?
    What would happen if you didn't use them in that way and
    people saw the way you really are? Would you fear people's
    reactions?

    *When I first started out, I used
    makeup and clothes for affirmation from
    people. When I meet new people I do
    hide behind clothes/makeup/etc. I haven't
    been wearing makeup lately & sometimes it
    makes me feel less feminine.*

10. Or do you hide behind clothes that you would call 'frumpy'
    because you feel safer that way – other women are
    unthreatened, feel superior and are nicer. And you don't have
    to worry about men rejecting you because you don't think
    they'll notice you at all?

    *Not really. I don't think I ever have.
    When I'm frumpy it's a lazy day
    but I feel unfeminine & like people
    think I'm a scruff.*

3

The Woman God Sees

We've thought about the woman you see when you look at yourself and how you feel about her. You've asked yourself whether you'd call her beautiful, lovable or significant. But what would you *LIKE* to hear in answer to those questions? Not what you think/ fear the answers could/ should be but what, if you allowed yourself to dream, they would be. Deep down, would you like to be beautiful, to look lovely, to be noticed, and highly thought of? Would you like to be universally loved – for people to praise, appreciate and desire you? Would you like to matter – to have something to contribute that would be worthwhile and significant – to live a fulfilled life?

1.   "Am I beautiful?"   *I want to be pure*

Yes. As beautiful as a sunrise at dawn. Captivating. Desirable. A natural beauty where people stop and stare; not just on the outside, but inside too.
I want to be feminine.

2.   "Am I lovable?"

Yes. I want people to really want to be my friend for people to love being in my presence. To value me and take note of me. I don't want to be left out or seen as "mamma Crawley" or "frumpy".

3.   "Do I matter? Do I have a worthwhile and significant purpose for being alive?"

Yes. I'd like to be able to have a go at anything and not feel so awkward/ "frumpy" in myself. I want to know who I am & where I'm going & for people to know me as driven, passionate.

"Who am I?" and "What's the point of my life?" are pressing questions that we gather answers to over the course of our lives from a number of different sources. But we need to stop and ask ourselves: Who's actually right about me? Who should I listen to and believe? 21st century media – the TV, magazines and newspapers; my background; the government; my doctor; my boss; my friends; my education; my family; myself? ...GOD?

Truth would be a level against which everything else could be measured. **But does that absolute, genuine, actual, factual verdict on you exist *anywhere*?**

The Bible says that it does and that God is the only one who *never* lies (Romans 3:4). And as our Creator, it makes a lot of sense that He would be the one to know who we are and why we're here. What if He saw you and gave His opinion? According to the Bible, He sees you and He says:

> *"I am the Lord; there is no God besides me.⁵ I stretched out the earth upon the waters.⁶ But long before I laid down earth's foundations, I had you in mind, had settled on you as the **focus of my love**.⁷*
>
> *I formed your inward parts and knit you together in your mother's womb.⁸ You are **fearfully and wonderfully made**.⁹ In my image.¹⁰ And I brought you forth on the day you were born.¹¹*
>
> *I know everything about you.¹² I know your every thought.¹³ I am familiar with all your ways.¹⁴ Every moment I know where you are.¹⁵I know what you are going to say even before you say it.¹⁶ My thoughts about you are **innumerable**. They outnumber the grains of sand!¹⁷ Thoughts of peace and not of evil.¹⁸*
>
> *I am enthralled by your **beauty**.¹⁹ I so **loved** you that I sent my only Son into the world.²⁰ He came so that you may **have and enjoy life**, and have it **in abundance (to the full, till it overflows)**.²¹ He died to bring you back to me.²² If you believe Him and accept Him, you have the right to **become my child**. You are reborn!²³ Recreated in Christ Jesus that you may do those good works which I predestined (**planned** beforehand) for you (taking paths which I **prepared** ahead of time) that you should walk in them (living the **good life** which I prearranged and made ready for you to live).²⁴*
>
> *For I know the plans I have for you, plans to **prosper** you and not to*

harm you, plans to give you **hope** *and a* **future.** *25 Instead of shame and dishonour, you will inherit a double portion of* **prosperity and everlasting joy.** *26 Nothing will be able to separate you from my* **love.** *27 I will* **keep** *you from all harm.* *28 Each day I* **carry** *you in my arms.* *29 And you will dwell in my house* **forever.** *30*

Call to me and I will **answer** *you.* *31 I can do anything—* **FAR MORE** *than you could ever imagine or guess or request in your wildest dreams!* **"** *32, 33*

Wanting To Be Beautiful

"Am I beautiful/ lovable/ significant?" God is saying that we are. His words speak of our value and potential. He calls us beautiful, tells us that even before there was a world, He loved us and had plans for our lives. Whatever your experience has been, you were no accident but a beautifully planned and packaged *gift* to your parents (Psalm 127:3 NLT).

When you asked yourself those three questions earlier, were you hesitant or embarrassed about admitting that you would like to be beautiful, loved and significant? They may be buried under a lot of hurt and disappointment but those desires are planted deeply within us.

The Bible tells us all about God's perfection – His goodness, mercy, love, justice, fairness, holiness and righteousness. His attitudes and behaviour are beautiful. He has created an awe inspiringly beautiful universe. You were made to desire to be beautiful, to make things beautiful, to be an attractive, delightful woman because you were made to display God's beauty in a unique way.

Wanting To Be Loved

Like Adam and Eve, we were made to be known and deeply loved, to enjoy companionship and intimacy with God and each other. To this day *what a man desires is unfailing love* (Proverbs 19:22 NLT). And isn't it true? Deep in your heart do you long for **earth stopping, heart pounding, real,**

true love? The devotion of someone who will still love you even when you have revealed every single tiniest part of yourself to them? We want to be noticed, appreciated, romanced, called 'gorgeous' because we were made for no less than the true love we crave, the love of God.

Wanting To Be Significant

And each human being has been made unique, not to hide in shame but to flourish as their potential is given the full expression that it was made for. If you long to have purpose – for your life to count for something – it is quite simply because you were made to be **eternally and irreplaceably significant.** You were made *to have and enjoy life, and have it in abundance (to the full, till it overflows)* (John 10:10 AMP). You were made to **really live!**

The main part of this book is split into three sections: BEAUTIFUL, LOVED, REALLY LIVING, helping you see how these deep longings of humanity can be satisfied in your own experience! You will find out who God has made you to be, how to discover the good plans He had for your life before you were even conceived and how you can overcome the obstacles, opposition and hurts that have challenged you, to fulfill all it means to be you.

planned, designed, conceived,

individual, unique, purposed,

gifted, priceless, rescued,

purchased, forgiven, restored,

adopted, worthy, radiant,

altogether lovely, irresistible,

BEAUTIFUL

4

Fallen Women Fixed by God

Having relationships with human beings was so important to God that He gave Adam and Eve the freedom of choice. He could have made them love Him and behave perfectly but relationships are rich because we **CHOOSE** to know and love, **CHOOSE** to be known and loved. And God wanted real, proper friendship, not to work the remote controls of a race of robots.

Adam and Eve could make decisions for themselves. Choose to do what God told them to – or not. And in choosing to rebel against Him, sin entered humanity so we *fall short of the glory of God* (Romans 3:23 NIV). We have seen that falling short of God's glory has made us live rooted in feelings of shame, guilt and rejection.

The feeling that there is something wrong with us gets worse the more attention is drawn to it by all the promised ways to get us FIXED:

Fix 1 – Self Improvement Culture

This culture appeals to the drive in us to overcome the feeling that we're just not all we could be. It promises to make us desirable, confident, happy and successful, giving us the increased confidence, purpose and satisfaction we crave or at least to help us find them. There is a FIX offered for just about everything from diet gurus, body language experts, voice coaches, personal trainers, stylists and plastic surgeons for the body; education and travel to build mind and character; meditation retreats for the spirit; therapists to fix everything from our relationships with our pets to our partners; and beautiful and useful things to buy to perfect our homes.

Cue The Makeover...

We've all seen the makeovers. Instant fixes that provide no actual lasting solution. The cameras roll and a woman gets new clothes, makeup and hairstyle and she can seem like a new person. It's not just that she looks more attractive but we're faced with a more confident, happier person. Gone is the invisibility she was lost in. Suddenly we know that she's got an overwhelming potential – not just to look better – but hidden depths to who she really is and could be that are waiting to surface.

The cameras cut, the programme ends and real life takes over. Except we don't see the rain turn her ironed hair to frizz, the school phone about her child's disruptive behaviour, the Botox wear off or her credit card statement arrive. Life happens from minor irritations to major disasters.

We don't see the unhappiness, invisibility and lacking confidence creep back. Even a promotion in her work – something she loves and is good at – isn't enough to give her the real and lasting satisfaction she craves.

We don't see her stand in front of the mirror and see the way she feels about herself a few months later: unattractive, undesirable, incompetent.

What she needs is to find a way of giving that glimmer of potential its full expression regardless of how she looks and how life is going.

FIX 2 – The Positive Self Image / Worth / Esteem Thing

Pursuing beauty, popularity and success to make us feel less inferior doesn't make anyone 100% happy in their skin. It doesn't come close to filling the depths of our souls, sustaining us or making sense of all the uncertainties of life. However much work we do on ourselves, we just can't get rid of our own shame.

That's why for all the self improvement industry's rules and suggestions to live by and fail at, there's a growing trend towards saying: "Let's forget 'perfection'. Let's accept ourselves as we are. Let's take the pressure off."

**ESTEEM:
have good, high
opinion of; value;
respect;
approve; admire; like;
love...**

There is a backlash against the drive to self improve that encourages replacing it with 'self esteem', 'self worth' or 'positive self image'. **They're basically different ways of describing: 'having a good opinion of oneself'.**

They're recognising our inherent worth as a human being regardless of how we look/ what we do/ how other people rate us/ how life is going.

They're having a confidence and ease with ourselves that's unaffected by our mistakes, shortcomings or successes.

And they're having a self belief that allows us to be assertive and creative, free to make our own decisions without being self conscious and anxious about what people think.

So does the positive self image / worth / esteem thing really work?

There's no doubt that humans are extraordinarily diverse and intricately made, that our capacities are exceptional. But nonetheless, valuing ourselves just for who we are throws up a lot of questions:

*   Why should we think we have inherent worth as a human being?
*   What is the purpose in human beings anyway for them to have any particular value?
*   We know we have the capacity to mess up so why should we accept ourselves?
*   What's more, not everyone likes us. Not everyone esteems us at all! How do we know they're not the ones telling the truth?
*   And come to that, what actually is the truth?
*   Who's right?
*   Who should we listen to and believe? 21st century media, our background, our education, our family, OURSELVES???
*   Then there's the fact that however much we esteem ourselves, we know we've still got to face a harsh and hostile world where life can

be tough to say the least and where in some of the worst case scenarios, self love just wouldn't cut it. It wouldn't be enough to pull us through.

The freedom and confidence having a positive self image/worth/esteem promises is highly desirable. And in spite of the questions it throws up even appears obtainable up to a point. **But really it amounts to no more than mind over matter – choosing to esteem yourself and pretend that the heart of the problem of being fallen, the horrible shame, doesn't exist.**

Rescued By Love

In the end, whether we aim for perfection and work to improve ourselves, attempt to accept ourselves as we are or enter a negative pattern of trying to escape through a self destructive habit like drugs or alcohol, the results of the fall, and the shame, remain. Fallen humanity longs to be freed and we are surrounded by FIXES that have grown out of that. But they don't work. **We need a radical rescue.**

And that's exactly what God has provided. He has never given up on humanity. In spite of the fact we have rejected and all but forgotten Him, God has remained faithful to His creation. He has continued to be in love with every rebel who is birthed and to desire to walk through our lives and into eternity with each one of us.

He has made a way for the effects of the fall to be reversed. Fully, finally, forever FIXED. The perfect solution to every one of man's problems. The ultimate rescue plan:

JESUS!

We have had to face the fact that we will NEVER be able to get rid of our own shame. Even if we could take enough drastic steps that we felt we had got somewhere near physical and moral perfection, it wouldn't work. You can strive to make yourself skinny and fabulous looking but it won't get rid of your shame. You could live in the perfect house like the X's do but it wouldn't get rid of your shame. You could have the dream partner, the 'right' friends, popularity, an amazing car, all the money you could ever wish for, a great career, successful children, fame, power, global influence but none of it would get rid of your shame.

The only way you can be released from shame and find the love and acceptance you crave, the only way that you will ever **BECOME** _____Rachael_____ – discover who you truly are and
(insert your name here)
be able to become that woman, is to have the results of the fall reversed and your spirit brought alive by Jesus.

It's in Christ we find out who we are and what we are living for.

(Ephesians 1:11 MSG)

Jesus is the **ultimate and original superhero**, the One who rescues you with a love that takes you out of every captivity you have ever known. It is a love with a strength, a size and a power that breaks every chain that holds you and destroys every prison bar and dungeon door that seeks to hem you in. He alone can awaken and liberate all that is within you and take you:

FROM:	TO:
Confusion	Purpose
Fear	Hope
Regret	Contentment
Hurt	Joy
Feeling ugly	Being irresistible
Dark past	Bright future
Loneliness	Love
Giving up	Really living
Nobody	Somebody
Frustration	Fulfilment
Stress	Peace
Burdened	Strength
Striving	Satisfaction
Compromised	Free

I had these **ultimate results** listed on some publicity material I gave out at a workshop. Some of the women were looking at it together and I heard them saying: "It's all too good to be true." But you know? It's really not!

The beauty you crave in your broken life? The dancing you crave in your wounded walk? The safety you crave in your shattered world? The love you crave in your rejected heart? The blessings you don't even dare to begin to entertain a thought of in your guilty mess?

JESUS. You can find it all in Him. You can gather up all that you are, all you have, all you are not and think you could never become, give it to Jesus and allow Him to exchange it for all that He is.

Jesus looks at you – the woman He loves, the woman He went to hell and back (literally!) to rescue and He says to you:

> *"The Lord has… sent me to bind up and* **heal** *the broken hearted, to* **proclaim liberty** *to the [physical and spiritual] captives and the opening of the prison and of the eyes to those who are bound,… to* **comfort** *all who mourn,… to give them an ornament (a garland or diadem) of* **beauty** *instead of ashes, the oil of* **joy** *instead of mourning, the garment [expressive] of* **praise** *instead of a heavy, burdened, and failing spirit."*
> (Isaiah 61:1-3 AMP)

> **DIADEM = royal crown** For the daughter of the King.

He alone can make every ugly thing BEAUTIFUL. For the woman who asks Him to, the woman who wants to be rescued by love, He swaps everything bad for something good. He takes your shame away and replaces it with God's glory and beauty – God's own Spirit living inside you:

> *The [Holy] Spirit [Himself* **indwelling your innermost being and personality**]…. *that you may be filled [through all your being] unto all the fullness of God [may have the richest measure of the divine Presence, and become a* **body wholly filled and flooded with God Himself**]!*
> (Ephesians 3:16, 19 AMP)

If you've had enough of things the way they are, you want to become all God's made you to be and do all He's planned, you can hand over your shame and ask for it to be replaced with the beauty, glory and Spirit of God. You can ask that you would be restored to God's original design as all that is within your being comes alive so you can **BECOME** ___Rachael___ .

(insert your name here)

*"You're **beautiful** from head to toe, my dear love,"*

Yes! That's every part of **YOU**, _Rachael_ ,
that God's talking about...

(insert your name here)

*"**beautiful** beyond compare"*

...that's no more inferiority...

*"absolutely **flawless**"*

(Song of Solomon 4 MSG)

...that's altogether lovely.

A BEAUTY: a very attractive woman, an outstanding example of its kind, the combination of all the qualities of a person or thing that delight the senses and mind.
Collins Dictionary

5

So Beautiful

How does it make you feel to think that God calls **YOU** beautiful? Do you imagine that this kind of 'beauty' has only got to do with some spiritual inner loveliness that He appreciates? Well, God loves the inside – the mind, emotions and spirit of the woman He's made. But He also loves the physical body – so much that He desires to replace your shame with His own glory, living inside you Himself.

And that has to begin to change what you feel when you look in the mirror. Not only is your body of immense value to God but the outside is absolutely beautiful to Him.

We've been fed a lie that looking like what the world calls attractive is what determines our value as a person. That can make being beautiful on the outside seem shallow and unspiritual. But that is just because we are so limited in how we understand things. God's view of beauty is far, far bigger than the world's prescribed size 0, flawless standards. The extent of variety that God has made goes far beyond what we even understand by the word 'creativity'. He calls us beautiful because He made us and He likes what He made. And that's what our value rests on – being the creation of God, the ultimate artist, creator, designer. Full stop. We are His design.

As God completed each step of Creation, He was continuously happy with what He made (Genesis 1). There was nothing He felt a bit disappointed with. He was thrilled with all of it. He didn't single out certain animals or plants and say that they were less than His best. God can only ever do His best. He cannot make a mistake. He cannot do a bad job. And that's the God who made YOU.

That means that it would be wrong to say that only inner beauty matters because our looks were specially designed by God. You really are physically beautiful to Him. He loves your smile, the shape of your nose, your eyes, hair, curves. They were all His idea. When you begin to look at it like that, you realise just how special and interesting you really are. God bothered to design you. When He thought of you, He went ahead and made you a reality. He didn't decide you were a bad idea – He doesn't have bad ideas. **He didn't opt to leave you out**. He gave you life.

When I started to get to know God properly, He would tell me how much He loved what He had made – my curly hair, the colour of my eyes, my 'wonky waist' (the curves aren't quite symmetrical) and that He took delight in my thoughts and ideas. There was no way I could have thought up things like that – they certainly weren't views I'd *ever* had of myself.

When God told me that He loved my 'wonky waist' and 'curly hair' I was completely shocked. My waist wasn't really a big deal – just not quite 100% symmetrical. I accepted it but viewed it as something of a flaw. I had absolutely hated my hair over the years and even been through a phase, as a child, of hitting myself over the head with my hairbrush when I lost my temper and couldn't get it to look right. But God loved even these little things about me. He'd made them and He actually liked them. That meant that I had to start to look at myself in a different light.

I learnt that we have got to be open to being loved as we are and accept that it's not a concession that God is making. We need to remember that God doesn't have model beauty vs. the non model variety. **We are beautiful, not by comparison with other women, not on a scale of 1-10 but simply because God says so.**

Beautiful As A Woman

One of the key things about our bodies is that they're the bodies of women. God has made us **WOMEN** and it matters to Him that we feel **ATTRACTIVE AS WOMEN**, not just as spiritual beings devoid of gender. He showed me this one day after I'd been shopping. A string of condescending assistants, frustrations of not being able to find the right size and stunning shoppers in the changing rooms had made me feel inferior, less than other women and horrible about myself. I felt so unattractive and when I was talking to God about it, He seemed to be saying that I never look inferior to anyone. He told me to look at Song of Solomon 4:5 which I discovered says:

> Your **BREASTS** are like the twin fawns of a gazelle feeding among the lilies.
>
> (Song of Solomon 4:5 NLT)

I was blown away by God so specifically appreciating me as a woman. It was reassuring and wonderful to know that feeling attractive as a woman, which had really mattered to me, is important to God too.

God uses body language when He describes how beautiful we are to Him:

> "How beautiful you are, my beloved, how beautiful! Your **eyes** behind your veil are like doves. Your **hair** falls in waves, like a flock of goats frisking down the slopes of Gilead. Your **teeth** are as white as sheep, newly shorn and washed. They are perfectly matched; not one is missing. Your **lips** are like a ribbon of scarlet. Oh, how beautiful your mouth! Your **cheeks** behind your veil are like pomegranate halves – lovely and delicious. Your **neck** is as stately as the tower of David, jewelled with the shields of a thousand heroes. Your **breasts** are like the twin fawns of a gazelle, feeding among the lilies… **YOU ARE SO BEAUTIFUL MY BELOVED, SO PERFECT IN EVERY PART**."
>
> (Song of Solomon 4:1-7 NLT)

This is such an intimate appreciation of our physical bodies.

Fixed To Be Feminine

God made us male and female. He chose to make you a woman not a man by design, on purpose, for a purpose! But many of us have, at times, been less than happy to be the gender we are. The same devil who was out to destroy Eve wants to do the same to us. He's done everything possible since you were a child to keep you from developing into the person God's made you to be and that's included messing up what it means to be a woman.

The devil makes girls fearful of developing into women at puberty and feel embarrassed and ashamed. He has fuelled a lie that women are somehow inferior to men and many women have been badly abused, in differing ways, specifically because they are female. It's led to all sorts of behaviours in us: using our femininity in manipulative ways or trying to get rid of it altogether. We may have behaved like weak, crying victims, been sexually overt, hidden our sexuality or become hard and masculine.

But none of that is God's plan. With God there's no inequality – superiority or inferiority – but rather femininity and masculinity – those things which are specific or distinct to women and men. God doesn't discriminate – as far as He is concerned women and men, each individual human being, all have a great deal to contribute that is of equal value. It was to **both Adam and Eve** He spoke when He told them to go forth, multiply and take authority over the world (Genesis 2:28).

It's time we were unashamed of our womanhood, stopped wondering why we had to be born women and appreciated all that it means to be God's girls. When you hear the word 'feminine' immediate associations probably come to mind. But, what comes to God's mind? Ask Him: "What does it mean to be fixed to be feminine? To be your daughter instead of a son?"

You may want to turn away from the attitude you've had to being a woman and ask God to restore your femininity and heal the hurt knowing that His heart for you **BECOMING** ___Rachael___, is that you
(insert your name here)

become the WOMAN He made you to be.

6

"But I Don't Feel Beautiful"

"It Can't Be True"

Beautiful inside, outside and in every way – does it seem as if everything in you is rising up with objections to what God says about you?

You may be saying: "But I'm ordinary – I'm nothing special or outstanding." "I have an insecure/ inconsistent/ boring personality." "I have average/ common/ ordinary looks."

You may be thinking: "But I have flaws." "My feet are different sizes. I have scarring. My hair's thin. I'm fat. I have anger/addiction/envy etc. problems." Or you may read that and think: "What a whinger. Those things are nothing. I have BIG 'flaws' compared."

God says He loves and accepts you so if you agree with Him, you can no longer hate and reject yourself. But it may feel very difficult for you to turn around and say: "OK – you're happy with my height so I will be too!" The reality is that there are all the voices belonging to other people, the media and ourselves that don't agree with God's opinion and there are feelings inside us we feel won't go away however hard we try to believe God. You're probably hyper critical of yourself because for so long you've wanted to be protected from the negative reactions of other people.

Your natural response may be to say: "But God, it's not true!" because you're used to rejecting people's compliments, so that you can do the rejection and they can't hurt you. Or you may be inclined to say: "Whatever!" accepting it but taking it lightly because you know all about compliments – few are genuine – there's often an ulterior motive behind them. Or you may want to say: "You don't really" hoping that He'll say it again because you feel there's something very immodest about accepting a compliment. Or perhaps you just don't feel that God's opinion is enough – you feel that until the world loves you, and you're acceptable in worldly terms, you won't rest.

What is your reaction to what God says about you?

Doubting God's Love

It may be that you have trouble trusting God's love because you've had a hard time in your life and wondered how God could have subjected you to so much disappointment and heart ache.

But could it be that the same harsh critic (you!) who criticises your reflection in the mirror and sees herself through a variety of taunting voices and unflattering words, looks to God and sees Him, not as He is, but as her own projection of Him? We have a tendency to think that God's created in the image of fallen man with motives and ways that simply aren't His. But the Bible is clear: God loves you with PERFECT LOVE. **He is LOVE.**

So if God is only ever good and loving where has He been the whole time you've believed other things about Him and yourself? Could it be that He's been right there loving you? Could it be that when little things have touched your heart, that was God offering His love? Could it be that His arms were reaching out to you in your darkest hours? Could He be saying: *"I created you and have cared for you since before you were born"*? (Isaiah 46:3 NLT).

A friend told me about a woman who was receiving prayer for healing from the hurts of her childhood. She'd often been locked in a cupboard as a child and the person praying asked her where she felt Jesus had been during these times. The counsellor's mobile phone rang at this moment. This never normally happened because she always switched it off before sessions with clients but on this occasion she must have forgotten. The woman recognised the ring tune and said that it was the exact tune that used to go through her mind when she was in the cupboard. And there, she felt, was the answer to the question – Jesus had been there all along singing, comforting her in the darkness. And she received great healing of those painful memories through that realisation. Where has Jesus been your whole life? If there are particularly painful memories, ask Him where He was during them.

Choice

For literally years, I didn't believe that God loved me at all. Circumstances were difficult and I didn't think that I could see any sign of God's love for me. I didn't doubt that God was love or that He loved everybody else. I honestly believed that He'd made a massive mistake with me and was taking out His disappointment. Thank God I came to see the terrible lies that I lived in.

I knew God was real and that had big implications. It meant that I could never escape from Him because even if I turned my back on Him, He'd still be there. I believed in eternal life too, that one day I would face Him. And even if God didn't like me, I wanted an eternity in Heaven rather than Hell. When I considered that, I knew that I could hardly get to Heaven and have it out with God: one human woman versus the God of the Universe! No, I was going to get there, fall into His arms and receive His praise for running and finishing the race well. So I made a **CHOICE**. I told God that although I felt hated and abused by Him and that I had no evidence of its truth, I was going to **CHOOSE** to believe that He did love me because it said so in the Bible. That choice to believe what the Bible said changed everything for me.

Job had real faith in a powerful God but he was confused why this God seemed to cause him to suffer. He was afraid of a God he saw as mean and unfair, a God hurting him for the sake of it. He'd tried to be good but he was very much like many of us – he judged God's ways believing he knew a better path that would be fair. But God reminded him of His power and Job's mere humanity: *"Do you have an arm like God's and can your voice thunder like his?"* (Job 40:9 NIV). So Job repented for questioning God's sovereignty and justice and acknowledged His great power and perfect fairness: *"I know that you can do all things no plan of yours can be thwarted. You asked: "Who is this that obscures my counsel without knowledge?" Surely I spoke of things I did not understand, things too wonderful for me to know"* (Job 42:2-3 NIV).

Calling God A Liar

We have a CHOICE whether we accept what God has to say about us, whether we will CHOOSE to agree with Him or not.

I grew up constantly trying to make myself look 'right' but was often frustrated by feeling that I looked all 'wrong'. I didn't even know specifically what I didn't like – one minute it was my hair, the next the proportions of my body or the look of my clothes.

As I increasingly knew and experienced that God loved me and that He saw me as beautiful, I began to feel happier about myself to the extent that if anyone had asked, I would probably have said that I was happy in my skin. God found me lovely and it did make me feel better but I still didn't reach, what I perceived were, the world's standards of beauty and success. There was still a niggling sense inside me that I was a failure and couldn't be happy with myself until I did reach them. Sounds like shame?!

I was redeemed, fixed by Jesus, full of God's glory, yet I still walked in a certain amount of shame and my unbelief was actually a major insult to God.

God sees us. He loves us. He calls us beautiful. He highly values our uniqueness. Do we have any right to disagree? Because if we do, we effectively call God a liar!

> *"Destruction is certain for those who argue with their Creator.* **Does a clay pot ever argue with its maker?** *Does the clay dispute with the one who shapes it, saying, "Stop, you are doing it wrong!" Does the pot exclaim, "How clumsy can you be!" How terrible it would be if a newborn baby said to its father and mother, "Why was I born? Why did you make me this way?"*
>
> *This is what the Lord… says:* **"Do you question what I do? Do you give me orders about the work of my hands?** *I am the one who made the earth and created people to live on it. With my hands I stretched out the heavens."*
>
> (Isaiah 45:9-12 NLT)

We must remember that **what God says about us is not just an opinion, just a compliment, just fatherly bias or husbandly devotion.** What God says about us is the TRUTH. GOD IS TRUTH. He cannot lie. He hates lies and deceit. He hates flattery. The words spoken by God are the only absolute TRUTH there is. The Bible says that God is the **only one** who never lies (Romans 3:4).

And He created you to feel good and right about yourself. It is the devil who wants you to feel all wrong. He wants you to feel shame, guilt and condemnation. And when you don't agree with God, you not only call God a liar, you AGREE WITH THE DEVIL! So:

> *Stop quarrelling with God! If you agree with Him, you have peace at last, and things will go well for you.*
>
> (Job 22:21 NLT)

Accepting You The Way God Does

If you've been struggling to accept what God's saying to you about who you really are – tell Him. Perhaps there are parts of you that you can come to accept and love as God does. But there may be other things about yourself that you would love to see healed and transformed. Tell God and ask Him for healing. Tell Him you want a new beginning – to be able to believe and know the truth about who He is and who you are.

What happens if you look at the cross and see Jesus hanging there but then you see yourself hanging there too? You see the truth. That's what happened. You and I deserved to hang on the cross, to be branded guilty. We deserved to face our shame, to feel the humiliation, to be stripped and mocked. But Jesus took it all upon Himself. He was punished in our place. He took our shame. He suffered our humiliation.

When you realise that your shameful sinful nature – that rebel who opposes God who is found in every single one of us – was put to death, nailed to the cross with Jesus, and all your sin – past, present, future is taken care of – then your real life can begin. You will **BECOME** ___Rachael___.

(insert your name here)

God accepts you as you are and you can too. It has nothing to do with your performance. Nothing to do with anything you could ever do. You have got to forgive yourself the same way that God has forgiven you.

Juan Carlos Ortiz discovered the importance of this. For many years he suffered from terrible migraines. He was prayed for by many people. He went to the best doctors in Argentina, North America and Europe, even to a psychiatrist, but the headaches just got worse. One day when he was reading his Bible, it became clear to him that he didn't accept himself at all. God said to him:

"You know, Juan Carlos, I know you better than you know yourself. Actually you are worse than you think. But I have accepted you – not because of your performance, but because of the blood of Jesus. Although I know all your wrongs, I have forgiven them all, right up until the day you die. Unless you forgive yourself all your wrongs – not just some of them, but all – and unless you promise yourself that you are always going to forgive yourself, you will never have peace with yourself."[34]

When Ortiz made peace with himself, believed that he really was fully, finally, forever FIXED by Jesus, the migraines ceased and never returned.

Think back to Chapter 1 when you imagined telling yourself what you thought of her. Imagine that again – yourself facing you. What if you hug yourself this time? Say to yourself: "I forgive you. I've been so angry with you, I've wanted to punish you. But I am so sorry and I forgive you for the past, the present and the future." Make peace with yourself. And finally say to yourself: "God loves you _____*Rachael*_____ and that's good

(insert your name here)

enough for me: I accept and love you too. **And I think that you are beautiful."**

7

Seeing Beautiful

In complete contrast to God who NEVER lies, **the devil ONLY EVER lies** (John 8:44). He has been feeding us lies all our lives, determined that we will never know the truth and experience it. We are made of three parts – body, soul (= emotions, mind and will (that part of you that has desires and makes choices)) and spirit. Although we are indwelt by God's Spirit, bringing our own spirits fully alive, our minds are full of old mindsets and thought patterns.

Our minds have been assaulted with filth and we desperately need them to be renewed to God's truth – to start to see things the way He does, to think thoughts in line with His. Contrary to popular opinion, it's not actually the 'normal' habitat of our minds for them to be worried, insecure, indecisive, troubled and hopeless. It seems like everyone takes feeling like that for granted but it's not what we've been made for.

> *There must be* **a spiritual renewal of your thoughts and attitudes** (Ephesians 4:23 NLT). *Let God transform you into a new person by* **changing the way you think**.
> (Romans 12: 2 NLT)

Ask Him that your mind would be radically renewed; that you would see, think and understand His way from now on so you will be able to live His thoughts into words and actions.

A New Mirror

For our minds to begin to be renewed and the lies to be replaced with the truth, we need to start reading the Bible with eyes open in wonder and belief:

45

*Your eyes are windows into your body. If you **open your eyes wide in wonder and belief**, your body fills up with light. If you live squinty – eyed in greed and distrust, your body is a dank cellar. If you pull the blind on your windows, what a dark life you will have!*
(Matthew 6:22-23, MSG)

Looking in the Bible is like looking in a new mirror.

There are wonders to discover in its pages about the woman you truly are, about the ULTIMATE MAKEOVER – the SALVATION – that took place when you accepted all Jesus had done for you in dying and being resurrected. SALVATION's not just about being forgiven. It's the greatest exchange ever. It's one word that includes every single benefit and blessing that God has for you – the meeting of every single one of your needs.

Jesus has taken your weakness for His strength, your sickness for His health and healing spiritually, mentally, emotionally, physically, financially and socially. Everything is found in Jesus. There is NO problem that can't be solved, NO difficulty that can't be overcome, NO advance that can't be made. And it is all for YOU! With His love.

To **BECOME** ___Rachael_____, you will need to spend time
                        (insert your name here)
really getting to grips with the truth about your identity. You need to put, see and speak yourself into the Bible. Every promise of blessing and protection is yours.

You can put your name in every promise. It's not adding to the Bible. When God wrote it, He had your name in mind. Your very own name is throughout the Bible:

_____ **is**_____ , **has**_____ , **can do**_____ etc.
        (insert your name here)

As you read the Bible, it may help to underline everything that speaks of who you are/ what you can do and what is yours in Christ. If you go to EXTRAS at the end of the book, you'll find some examples in YOUR NEW MIRROR.

You have got to begin to think of yourself the way you really are, the way

God describes you in the Bible. You are dead to sin. Your record of sin has been wiped out by God. This isn't mind over matter but supernatural thinking. It's living in what's true since the moment you met Jesus. **You can't any longer think of yourself as a rotten sinner but instead a born again saint.**

You're not going to become a saint in a few years once you've read the Bible a number of times and done some good things for the church. You were made one in a moment. The moment you allowed the blood of Jesus to wipe out your sin. You can't get any cleaner. Your spirit is good through and through. Sin is out of character for you now. It just needs your mind to catch up with what has happened in your spirit. You no longer need to see yourself as a thief or gossip or whatever. The Holy Spirit lives within you – you can know what it is to be empowered to be different from the way you have been.

The devil will keep telling you that you are what you're not. But you've got to deny the assertions and rest in your true identity. Thinking of yourself as a sinner, always remembering the bad you've done, robs you and it doesn't honour God. Start living in your forgiven – ness. Insist on your true identity. Live free from the past and drop your baggage off once and for all – you don't have to keep hauling it around with you.

The way you see yourself is what you will expect from yourself and the way you'll perform. Your vision of you has got to match God's. Otherwise you will constantly try to change yourself and fail.

Read the Bible, see yourself the way you truly are and start living like it's all true. Start living like that woman it describes who is ALTOGETHER LOVELY. Compare this picture on the next page: *"I Am Altogether Lovely"* with the previous one: *"I Feel Ugly"*.

"I AM ALTOGETHER LOVELY"

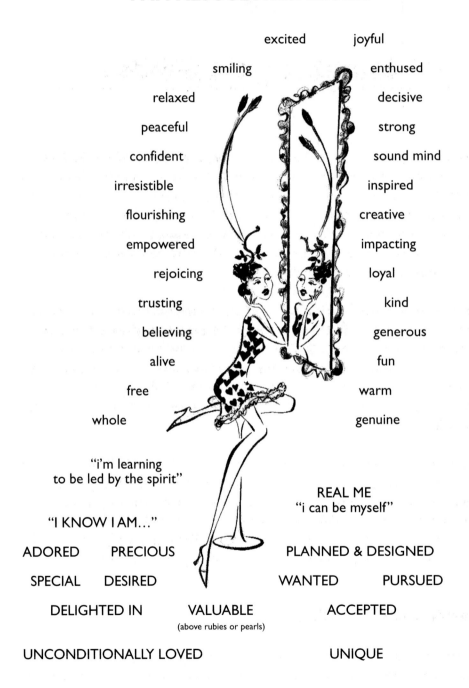

excited   joyful

smiling   enthused

relaxed   decisive

peaceful   strong

confident   sound mind

irresistible   inspired

flourishing   creative

empowered   impacting

rejoicing   loyal

trusting   kind

believing   generous

alive   fun

free   warm

whole   genuine

"i'm learning
to be led by the spirit"

REAL ME
"i can be myself"

"I KNOW I AM..."

ADORED   PRECIOUS   PLANNED & DESIGNED

SPECIAL   DESIRED   WANTED   PURSUED

DELIGHTED IN   VALUABLE   ACCEPTED
(above rubies or pearls)

UNCONDITIONALLY LOVED   UNIQUE

8

Speaking Beautiful

It's time to turn your thoughts into words and **speak the TRUTH**. It says in Romans 10:10 that *with the mouth confession is made unto salvation* (NKJV). That means that we possess all that Jesus has done, by faith, as we make our speech agree with what God says in the Bible. The devil wants to rob us of our Salvation but we don't have to let him. Jesus has won freedom, rest and victory for you in every area of your life. And you can live in it – in peace and joy and not in turmoil.

So how does this work in real life? Money is tight and seems to be getting tighter and you say: *"God is able to make all grace abound towards me, that I, always having all sufficiency in all things, may have an abundance for every good work"* (2 Corinthians 9:8 NKJV). You can dare to proclaim: "God has promised that I will always have all sufficiency in everything." That is part of your Salvation and you can expect God to provide for your needs as He has said He will.

Every problem we come up against requires us to confess God's answer to the problem. The more we say what God says, the more we will experience the fullness of our Salvation. Jesus is the high priest of our confession (Hebrews 3:1). He sits at the right hand of God and represents us. He listens to what we say and each time our words agree with God's words, He can present them to the Father with the guarantee that they will produce fruit in our lives.

Lies Versus The Truth

"Thank you, legs. I want you to know I appreciate you. You have carried Ruth safely everywhere she needed to go – and now you have brought her to me. Thank you legs!" That was the way Derek Prince prayed for his fiancée Ruth's very painful legs. When she questioned this unusual method of praying, he told her that he had been "unsaying something" she might have said about her legs. She remembered a scene in the loos at school, more than 30 years previously, when she was fifteen or sixteen. She says: "Another girl had come in and stood combing her hair. I looked at her shapely legs, and at my own heavy calves and ankles, and said, "I hate my legs!" In effect, I had placed a curse on my own legs!" The curse was lifted and Ruth was healed.[35]

Our mouths can speak blessings or curses. Our words carry either life-giving or destructive force (Proverbs 18:21). Many of us have placed curses on ourselves in the things we've said or been cursed by things that have been said about us. We can see something bad and a seed of negativity or fear drops into our minds.

To help you become aware of the lies we can end up living in, you have a chart on the next page with columns marked 'LIES' and 'TRUTH'. It gives some common types of lie with God's truth beside it.

Ask the Holy Spirit to reveal any lies about yourself that you have been living in as if they were the truth. There are probably lots in your life and this may be a time God wants to highlight a number or just one thing specifically. Add them to the chart and ask God what His truth is. Some of the verses here may be appropriate or the ones in EXTRAS at the end of the book.

ISSUE	LIES	TRUTH
Illness	"I'm sick. The doctors say I'm sick. It's the diagnosis I have. All the statistics point to the fact that I will always have this condition."	"I am not a statistic. God is controlling my life and all things are possible with Him (Matthew 6:26). Sickness, I'm not putting up with you. I command you to leave me in the name of Jesus. *By His stripes I have been healed and made whole.*" (Isaiah 53:5 AMP)
Inherited Problems	"Cancer runs in our family. It killed my mother and grandmother. This is my lot in life. What hope have I got?"	"My family tree does not dictate my life anymore because I've been adopted into God's family (Ephesians 1:5). Galatians 3:13–14 says that Jesus became a curse for me so that I might receive God's blessings. The blood of Jesus has saved me and I proclaim the curse of cancer is broken over my family in Jesus' name. *I pray that I will prosper in all things and be in health.*" (3John 1:2 NKJV)
	"My family is so dysfunctional. What hope do I have with my son? He's appalling and I can see him turning out just like his father."	"*As for me and my family we will serve the Lord* (Joshua 24:15). *I fear God and so His righteousness will be with my son: From everlasting to everlasting The Lord's love is with those who fear Him, And His righteousness with their children's children.*" (Psalm 103:17 NIV)

[handwritten margin note: dad – depression & negative]

Lack of Confidence	"I have no confidence. Everyone else can do everything. I'm just incompetent."	"I am a child of God, indwelt by His own Spirit and *I can do ALL THINGS through Christ who strengthens me.*" (Philippians 4:13 NKJV)
Failure	"How long have I been struggling with this thing? Breakthrough will never come for someone like me."	*"Amid all things I am more than a conqueror and gain a surpassing victory through Him who loved me."* (Romans 8:37 AMP)
	"I have failed so many times. I fail at exams, interviews, relationships, even card games. I was born to fail! I'm a loser."	*"I have victory wherever I go* (2Samuel 8:6 AMP). *It is the Lord who goes before me; He will [march] with me; He will not fail me or let me go or forsake me. I will fear not, neither become broken [in spirit – depressed, dismayed, and unnerved with alarm]."* (Deuteronomy 31:8 AMP)
Appearance	"I'm fat so I'm ugly."	*"My God is my glory and my beauty."* (Isaiah 60:19 AMP)
Future	"Everyone's always told me that no man will ever want to marry me so why would they? I mean if I was attractive someone would at least ask me out."	*"My beauty within and without is absolute* (Song of Solomon 7 MSG) and God has a good plan for my life – *to prosper me and not to harm me, to give me hope and a future."* (Jeremiah 29:11 NIV) What does God say about your future? He will begin to tell you if you ask Him. There is more about that in

		the chapters in 'REALLY LIVING' but for now know that what other people have said/ what you have feared is all finished in Jesus' name.
	"I'm scared of bad things happening."	*"No weapon that is formed against me shall prosper and every tongue that arises against me in judgment I do condemn. This is my heritage as a servant of the Lord."* (Isaiah 54:17 NKJV)
Identity	"My nickname's been 'Scaredy Kat' for as long as I can remember because I'm always so nervous about everything. It's not mean, it's affectionate. My sister even painted me a bowl with my nickname on that I eat my cereal out of every morning."	"I repent of walking in fear and I command you spirit of fear to leave me now in the name of Jesus. Holy Spirit, please fill me with the peace that Jesus died to give me. I proclaim that I do not have *a spirit of fear but of power, of love and of a sound mind."* (2 Timothy 1:7 NKJV) I have broken that bowl and thrown it away and I am telling everyone to stop calling me 'Scaredy Kat'. Do you have a nickname or possessions that describe the woman you are not? If you do, it's time to call an end to it. Ask people not to call you by the name anymore and destroy anything that reminds you of it.

the lies of my past etc [handwritten annotation]

Lack / Financial Problems	"I am at rock bottom. I have nothing. There is no way I can *ever* get out of this kind of debt."	Your bank statement may say it in black and white but that doesn't limit God. "My father is the owner of the entire universe. That makes my resources unending. Jesus has died so I will always have enough. As I live for God, I believe that He will get me out of this and *will generously provide all I need. Then I will always have everything I need and plenty left over to share with others.*" (2Corinthians 9:8 NLT)
God's Love	"I'm scared that God will get tired of me."	"*I am persuaded beyond doubt (am sure) that neither death nor life, nor angels nor principalities, nor things impending and threatening nor things to come, nor powers, nor height nor depth, nor anything else in all creation will be able to separate me from the love of God which is in Christ Jesus my Lord.*" (Romans 8:38-9 AMP)
Unpopular / Rejected	"Hardly anyone has ever liked me. I've been bullied and I'm afraid of more rejection."	"*I will not remain in constant dread of human oppression...God's name is the Lord Almighty and He has put His words in my mouth and hidden me safely within His hand. He says that I am His.*" (from: Isaiah 51:13-16 NLT) "*The Lord is for me, so I will not be afraid.*

		What can mere mortals do to me? *Yes, the Lord is for me; he will help me.* *I will look in triumph at those who hate me.* *It is better to trust the Lord* *Than to put confidence in people."* (Psalm 118:6-8 NLT)
Your Forgiven-ness	"I can't measure up."	*"I was His enemy, separated from Him by my evil thoughts and actions, yet now He has brought me back as His friend. He has done this through His death on the cross in His own human body. As a result, He has brought me into the very presence of God, and I am holy and blameless as I stand before Him without a single fault."* (Colossians 1:21-22 NLT)
ISSUES	**MY LIES**	**THE TRUTH**
	"I................	"I................

Everything demonic came on Jesus on the cross. Your past, the environment you grew up in – none of it has the right any longer to dictate your life. The repeated cycle of evil that comes through the generations is broken by Jesus. Those problems in your family tree, those demons that oppress through your family line, no longer have to be your reality. You don't have to live under that genetic threat of cancer, addiction, barrenness or whatever. You can proclaim the curse is broken over you and the next generations.

There's so much available to you because of Jesus. **Don't live ripped off.** As you begin to speak God's truth – positive, encouraging words of life and blessing – things will change, for the better, in your life. There is power contained in the words of the Bible.

Action!

1.   Repent of each of the things that have come to mind – of saying and believing things about yourself that weren't true and put you into agreement with the devil.

2.   Thank Jesus that on the cross He took every curse upon Himself and ask in the name of Jesus that you would be released from each one.

3.   Claim God's truth in place of each lie. As a child of God, empowered by the Holy Spirit, you have endless good things to believe and say about yourself! You could stand in front of the mirror and read out the truth about the woman you really are.

4.   Keep on claiming it. When you find yourself going back into old habits of thinking and speaking of yourself as the woman you are not – **speak that truth loud and clear**.

Be positive!
& don't be lazy!

9

Living Beautiful

No More Shame

We have got so used to living in shame, so stuck in this terrible trap of seeing ourselves through shame blurred eyes that it's hard to imagine living confidently as the women we truly are. Imagine walking into a room and not feeling any shame, not feeling at all uncomfortable/ inferior/ anxious/ insignificant or however else shame has made you feel at times in your life.

I want that!

The exciting thing is that we really can feel different, know for certain that Jesus has taken away our shame. It took time for this to become true for me but bit by bit, it has become more and more the reality of my life as I have come to see and believe that God delights in me. **He really takes pleasure in you and me.** It is the deepening knowledge of this that has transformed the way I feel when I look in the mirror.

I told you in chapter 6 how I knew and believed God loved me and that Jesus had taken my shame but I still felt I wanted to be well thought of by the world. It was when I finally realised the extent of what Jesus had done, the reality of the abundance of God – that He actually wanted to pour love on me that I changed. I had been to a meeting and had felt so uncomfortable, so full of shame, as if I was a repulsive being, that I knew I needed to get it sorted out. When I was praying, I told God that I wanted Him to enjoy me. I wanted that for God very badly. I hoped He could but I didn't realise how much He does. Before bed that night, He told me to look at Song of Solomon 7:6. I discovered that God found me not only enjoyable but an *utter delight*:

> *"Oh, how delightful you are, my beloved; how pleasant for utter delight!"*
> (Song of Solomon 7:6 NLT)

It's phrased in *The Message* as:

> *"Your beauty within and without is absolute."*
> (Song of Solomon 7, MSG)

The woman goes on to say:

> *"I am my lover's.*
> *I'm all he wants.*
> *I'm all the world to him!"*
> (Song of Solomon 7, MSG)

I realised powerfully that God really loved me. The knowledge of it had built in me over time but it was like the revelation in my heart suddenly came alive. I could see myself in my mind at that meeting, walking in with Jesus. He had His arm around me, He was looking after me and introducing me to people. He is the King – the *handsomest of men; every word from* His *lips is pure grace* (Psalm 45:2 MSG). I had no shame, no fear, just the desire that other people would be blessed by encountering Jesus in me.

I saw myself completely differently after that. When we realise the shame is gone, it alters our relationship with our bodies. I didn't see all the things that were wrong when I looked in the mirror. Instead I started to see a whole: myself. A whole that I actually felt right about. I began to see a person, through what before I had seen as a mess.

Comparing with other women and worrying about what people, including men, thought didn't seem to matter anymore. I didn't think I looked as peaceful and content as I could have and I suddenly wanted to look those things. I wanted to reflect the awesomeness of Jesus and all He'd done to make me truly alive. I wanted to look after the body that He'd given me and chosen to make His home in. I realised that I wasn't nurturing it as well as I could – it was the temple of the Holy Spirit – and I wanted to look after it. I needed some new clothes but I felt more relaxed about that than I had in the past. They didn't have to make up for the lack in me anymore. I was bowled over by the way God sees me and I wanted to see myself the same way. I had real freedom and I knew what it meant to be reborn.

A Woman's Life Changed

One woman I know had been fixed by Jesus – filled with God's glory – but she still lived in shame. She had had a weight problem for about twenty years and in her eyes it defined her. It crippled the way she saw herself, and her life, and prevented her from properly entering into so many things. Her life went on as normal – husband, children, commitments – but within it she believed that she was totally worthless.

Finally, the truth took a hold of her and she saw that in spite of the fact that she had weight to lose still, that had nothing to do with her being beautiful, valuable and significant. She stepped out of her sense of shame and everything felt different.

She was driving along listening to a programme about Afghanistan, on the radio, and suddenly realised that she was no longer in the prison cell of shame so she could go to Afghanistan if she wanted to. In fact, she could actually go anywhere, do anything, free and confident.

You Living Beautiful

So be encouraged! Whatever your personal situation, the way you have felt about yourself can be completely turned around. We no longer fall short of God's glory. Even if we slip up in our behaviour, the effects of the fall are still reversed in us.

The reality is that the shame has gone. The question is whether we will choose to live as if it has or whether we will live like enemies of the cross whose *glory is in their shame* (Philippians 3:18-19 NIV).

What is glory in your shame? Feeling better about yourself because you've squeezed into a smaller size skirt than usual, because you've got a bigger house than your neighbour, because you've got pregnant and your friend never seems to be able to hold a relationship together. It sounds shallow, horrible, even mean, but if we're honest, that is exactly the sort of thing shame does to us. The nearer we are to physical perfection, to having all the things the world says make us worth something, the better we feel about ourselves.

Living like that has become a habit but one that can be broken as we get our heads around the truth, see the way we really are, described for us in the Bible, and speak of ourselves as women who have this new identity.

Everyday, there should be this sense of appreciating yourself as a glorious being – a whole – spirit, soul and body. Everyday, you can look in that mirror and think: "I'm lovely because God has bestowed His glory and beauty." Everyday, you can enjoy the wonder of it, the love butterflies of knowing that you are loved and made lovely. Everyday, you can feel right and good about yourself, because of Salvation, your righteousness, Christ in you.

Everyday, you can value your body and make the most of it – doing your hair, wearing clothes you like as a celebration of you. It's not dressing up to make people notice you and look as good, or hopefully better than them, but actually luxuriating in being the woman you are, freeing you to appreciate them for being them.

Free from that painful emotion arising from that awareness of being unworthy, ridiculous and foolish (=shame), you can enjoy being worthy, lovely, full of God's glory because there is nothing foolish or ridiculous about you. When you fill your mind with that, you step out like that and you allow the Holy Spirit in you to begin to flow.

And you walk like it's true, talk like it's true, laugh like it's true and love like it's true.

Beauty is in the eye of the beholder and you have to allow the beholder to be the One who painstakingly made you, who loves you so much He gave everything to take away your shame and have a relationship with you. The One who NEVER looks at you like you're dirt, NEVER says anything discouraging, mean, spiteful, negative. In fact:

HIS WORDS ARE KISSES, HIS KISSES WORDS

(Song of Solomon 4 MSG)

Go to EXTRAS at the back of the book for some KISSES FOR YOU!

Ways To Live Genuinely 100% Happy In Your Skin

Yes! That is what I believe we can realistically aim for. I am talking about more than:

The World's Way

When women work on building self esteem and improving their approach to their bodies, they try to change certain attitudes. They may accept the reality of different body shapes so stop making comparisons with other women. They may stop criticising all the parts of themselves that they're unhappy with and focus on their physical assets instead. They may downplay the importance of physical appearance: "I'd love longer legs, smaller waist etc. but wouldn't we all? I don't dwell on it – I know other things in my life are more important and give me more fulfilment." Or "I've stopped trying to measure up to the images of perfection in the magazines. I've decided to focus on having a healthy body instead."

Deep down all this self acceptance is really just a surrender to shame. You considered your body image in some detail with the questionnaire in Chapter 2. FIXED by God, your shame is removed and the damage it's caused can all be healed. So in light of what you have learnt about who you really are, here are some ideas to help you love the body you're in:

1. See your body as a beautiful whole and not in terms of good and bad bits

You know that not only has God made every last inch of you and He calls it beautiful but that He has bestowed His own glory upon you. You can see your body as a whole now, not just in terms of the good and bad; be happy with yourself as a complete person and not in bits.

2. Swap the lies for the truth

Always. What negative things are you in the habit of thinking/ saying about yourself? "My…. is so ugly. It's so unfair I have… I can't wear… because of…" Instead, replace them with God's truth.

Learn to appreciate and give dignity to your body.

(1 Thessalonians 4:4 MSG)

Where you've been negative about parts of your body, cursing them like Ruth Prince's legs, apologise to your body and tell it positive things.

3. Get grateful to God for the way He has made you

Thank God for the body He made for you:

> *Thank you for making me so wonderfully complex!*
> *Your workmanship is marvellous – and how well I know it.*
> (Psalm 139:14 NLT)

4. Realise your value doesn't lie in looking fashionably slim, young and flawless

Many, many women are distressed about their weight and believe that if they could just lose some, then they'd be happy, then their lives would really be able to begin. This is a *total lie*. Being slim doesn't necessarily make you the 'right' shape. Or make you 100% symmetrical. Or give you a face you'd call 'pretty'. Or make your clothes look the way you want them to. It doesn't change the circumstances of your life and make you successful, happy and in control. It certainly doesn't GET RID OF THE SHAME. Only Jesus can fix you and replace your shame with His glory.

↑SO TRUE

5. Look after the temple

When you see how precious you are to God and that He lives in you, it matters that you look after the temple that you are and eating the healthiest food possible is a priority:

> *Whatever you eat or drink or whatever you do, you must do all for the glory of God.*
> (1Corinthians 10:31 NLT)

6. See ageing God's way

Death isn't the end. It's the beginning of Eternity. So we don't have to be afraid of getting old. Rather than despising old age, we need to change the way we view it and see the great, and equal, value of the different stages of life:

> *The glory of the young is their strength; the grey hair of experience is the splendour of the old.*
> (Proverbs 20:29 NLT)

7. Be careful around magazines

Stop allowing the magazines and self improvement industry to negatively affect you. They play on humanity's deep fears and if we let them, they can make us ever more critical and dissatisfied to the point where we feel that we have no right to be 'imperfect', that it's a disgrace when we could pay lots of money to make ourselves look 'better'. Magazines present a version of 'perfection' that has nothing to do with being the unique and beautiful woman you were made to be.

8. Copy the real supermodel celebrity

We like to have somebody to look up to and emulate. Think about it. We have the best. The only one who is perfect: Jesus. More and more you want to look radiant, relaxed, glowing, confident, content, assured because you want to reflect the awesomeness of Jesus and all He's done.

> All of us have had the veil removed so that we can be mirrors that brightly reflect the glory of the Lord.
> (2Corinthians 3:18 NLT)

9. And let all the other celebrities, models and women off the hook

We must stop joining in with criticism of other women. That's criticising God's creation. These women are beautiful to God and our desire for them should be that they know God and His love and purpose in their lives. Remember the woman God saw in you in Chapter 3? Those words are for all the other women in the world too (and men come to that).

Begin to see other women the way God does and be nice to, and about, them. They probably have worries and doubts about themselves. You know what that was like!

10. Quit competing and comparing

You know that you are unique and if you're going to enjoy and make the most of that, it means that you're going to have to appreciate the differences between you and other women and stop envying them. Imagine you are wearing a badge that says:

> "I am beautiful,
> lovely,
> valuable,
> precious,
> brilliant,
> fabulous,
> full of treasure and potential,
> gifted,
> spectacular
> ... AND SO ARE YOU!"

11. People will keep on being people

You're not going to completely escape judgment and criticism from others. But you can stop being controlled by it. God's opinion is what matters.

12. Your value doesn't depend on what any man thinks about you

When our glory is in our shame, it really matters that we're found attractive by men. We like to be the one who catches the eye of the most desirable man in the room. Failing that, even builders' wolf-whistles or attention from someone we don't find the least bit attractive can make us feel better about ourselves.

We can end up dressing to manipulate men's reactions to us and flirting our way through life. But your worth doesn't depend on what any man thinks about you. If men fall at your feet that doesn't raise your value and it's not lowered if they don't.

13. Stop using clothes to hide behind and control people's reactions to you

Your clothes no longer have to be relied on to speak for you. You can stop feeling they need to be perfect or expensive to make up for the lack you feel in yourself and to make you more desirable or acceptable. And you can stop hiding behind clothes that you would call 'frumpy' because you feel safer that way.

14. Wear it your way

Know that true style is *your* style, not what's put on you by someone else but what you're comfortable in. When you're really being you, that's when you'll be your loveliest. You have personal taste and unique flair. Begin to let that develop as you make decisions based on what you actually LIKE, not what someone else will like or what a magazine tells you to wear. This doesn't mean you dismiss fashion at all but use it the way you want to.

Getting dressed is about framing a masterpiece. And doing it with conviction – with the confidence to do it your way – is having style!

DISCOVERING YOUR STYLE
When I've done workshops with women, helping them discover and develop their personal style, they begin asking themselves a question: "What do I like?" because the first stage in finding your personal style – your own way with clothes and accessories, with decorating your house, planning a dinner party, or whatever – is getting in touch with your personal taste – your likes and dislikes.

That may sound terribly simplistic. But although there are some people who have a very strong idea of what they like, the large majority of us have, from our earliest years, been getting increasingly confused. We've absorbed the criticism, compliments and messages of media and culture to form a scrapbook in our minds that reflects what we think style is. And your scrapbook may or may not be reflective of your real tastes.

MAKING AN INSPIRATION BOARD
The aim is to begin to create a personal style scrapbook that is reflective of your own tastes, a collage of looks you love and might want to imitate.

1.   Ask: "What do I like the look of?" Begin broadly with any ideas that come to mind. They may be landscapes, films, paintings, a period in history. Jot them down.

2.   Next, get some magazines. If you don't have any already, try to find some with fashion pages and ads in. And don't forget about the newspaper (there are often pictures in the weekend supplements) and clothes catalogues, etc. etc. and tear out pictures of clothes, accessories, fabrics, makeup, you like and any other things you feel drawn to the appearance of. Source things from everywhere which appeal to your eye. It may be a style of writing, a page from an in-flight magazine, a

food wrapper, a book cover...

Get inspired. You may want to take a trip somewhere like the costume galleries at a museum, go to the library to look in some books and take photocopies, have a look on the internet, hire some films. Look for ideas everywhere you go. Look at postcards, greetings cards. Get colour swatches from paint shops and look at nature:

"It didn't start to come together for us until we began emulating Mother Nature's palette. Instead of thinking boiled sweets, we began to look at the sunset, an autumn tree, the fire and hey presto, things began to work."

– Trinny and Susannah[36]

Have a lot of fun! And do this ON YOUR OWN. Don't be limited or put off by anything. Don't even consider whether it would fit/suit you/be affordable. This is your opportunity not to say: "I'd have that if... I had more money, a different figure, a better social life to dress for, was a few decades younger, my husband would approve..." but your fantasy shopping trip!

DEFINING YOUR 'LOOK'

3.   Try to assess your 'purchases' a bit. You may find that there's a certain colour you've been drawn to again and again or a particular look. Analyse why you like something. Is it the hem or top length, the neckline, the fabric or decoration, a skirt shape or the work of a particular designer?

CREATING YOUR 'LOOK'

4.   Look at your cuttings. What looks do you love for casual, work, going out? Make a list of different occasions you have to dress for: evening, sport, at home, work etc. and plan your ideal wardrobe along the lines of the styles you're discovering you like.

"I often wear evening wear because that is my personality. I don't really do functional."

–Lulu Guinness
(Seen food shopping in M&S in a little black dress and stilettos).[37]

The appeal of women with defined personal styles: their visible knowledge of and contentment with being who they are.

– Hadley Freeman[38]

15. You are free to be creative without rules...

Get over the fear of getting it wrong. Laws have been made out of things that should be personal decisions! Just because Christian Dior said "a 'little black frock' is essential to any woman's wardrobe" doesn't made it a compulsory purchase for a really stylish woman. Get one if you like them. Don't if you don't. Who is Christian Dior that you should follow his instructions?

16 ....or the fear of judgment

Appreciate other people's creativity and be free to use your own without fearing criticism. Instead of thinking that what someone is wearing looks awful or ridiculous, live and let live: "I have my own style... AND SO DO YOU."

17. Enjoy clothes

It's not wrong to look attractive and make an effort. You can enjoy clothes as gifts from God. He is endlessly creative. He knows what's in the shops. So ask Him about a budget, pray at the hairdresser's, pray when you plan outfits and rely on the Holy Spirit to inspire your styling.

KNOW FIRST WHO YOU ARE AND ADORN YOURSELF
ACCORDINGLY.

– Epictectus

*Walk out into the fields and look at the wildflowers. They never primp or shop, but have you ever seen colour and design quite like it?... If God gives such attention to the appearance of wildflowers – most of which are never even seen – **don't you think He'll attend to you, take pride in you, do His best for you?** What I'm trying to do here is to get you to relax, to not be so preoccupied with getting, so you can respond to God's giving.*

(Matthew 6:28-32 MSG)

God hasn't invited us into a disorderly, unkempt life but into something holy and beautiful – as beautiful on the inside as the outside.

(1Thessalonians 4:7 MSG)

If You Take One Thing...

If I could get you to take just one thing from this part of the book, it is that you would see the truth about your identity. That you are beautiful.

FULL STOP.

When Jesus swaps your shame for His glory, in one split second beauty is bestowed. Your spirit is brought fully alive and it is good. You don't have a long, long, long way to go to become worthy. You'll never be able to earn more status with God than what you already have. You won't become a saint in the future when you've done something especially spiritual.

I used to see myself back down in the gutter every time I'd done something wrong, needing to crawl back to God's arms. But there's no more gutter for the DAUGHTER OF THE KING. No apprenticeship to be taken, no qualifying exams to be passed. Her diadem, that royal crown, is in place. It doesn't even slip. The shame and ashes are gone. Nowhere to be found. She is a saint. She is a princess. And the King's hand doesn't let her go.

Remember this!

You don't have to keep getting re-rescued. Or re-reborn. It doesn't strike midnight and you lose that *clothing of salvation* that makes you like a *bride with her jewels* (Isaiah 61:10 NLT).

So if you take just one thing, decide that you will accept your beautiful identity with a smile, enjoy it and live as if it's true.

It is true!!

*Let the saints be joyful in the **glory and beauty** [which God confers upon them].*
(Psalm 149:5 AMP)

accepted, invited, beloved,

valued, adored, desired

esteemed, pursued, romanced,

known, watched over,

cherished, nurtured,

protected, delighted in,

LOVED

10

The Ultimate Relationship

Just to recap the story of *BECOMING YOU* so far:

God created each of us unique, to feel right and good about ourselves. But shame makes us feel anything but. We end up hiding and performing and losing sight of who God's made us to be. But God has provided the ultimate rescue plan. Because Jesus was punished in our place, our old sinful nature has been crucified and our spirits have been reborn so that we can be daughters of God. No more shame – 100% BEAUTIFUL, filled with His Spirit to lead and empower us. We choose to open our eyes in wonder and believe that what God says is the truth, breaking our agreements with the devil, and agreeing with God instead. As we speak the truth, we find we become what we believe and we begin to enjoy **the ultimate relationship**...

Do you remember asking yourself what you would like to hear in answer to: "Am I lovable?" You know now that you are – extremely – because God says so and He speaks the truth. In this part of the book, **you are going to see how to have the ultimate relationship, the love affair with God, that means everything to you** *BECOMING* ___Rachael___ .
(insert your name here)

Called Into This Relationship
The Bible says that:

> *by Him [God] you were* **called into COMPANIONSHIP** *and participation with His Son, Jesus Christ our Lord.*
>
> (1 Corinthians 1:9 AMP)

That tells us that God is saying to you and me:

"I am CALLING *YOU* into companionship with my son, Jesus."

Not only have we been rescued by Jesus, but we have been rescued to become women who accompany Him, who spend time with Him, who are friends with Him. **This is our calling. The very reason for our existence!** The absolute heart of our purpose is to know and love God, to enjoy an intimate relationship with Him, with Jesus and with His Spirit.

Jesus said that the *goal and purpose* of His life was God (John 14:27 MSG). Paul felt the same:

> *"[My determined purpose is] that I may KNOW Him (Jesus) [that I may progressively become more deeply and intimately acquainted with Him, **perceiving and recognising and understanding the wonders of His Person** more strongly and more clearly]."*
>
> (Philippians 3:10 AMP)

But how on earth does this relationship work?

When it comes to advice about how to develop this relationship with Jesus, the answers always seem to be the same – "Read the Bible", "Pray", "Spend time with Him" – leaving you feeling unsure exactly what action to take. Do you ever hear people say that they've had an amazing prayer time, or really enjoyed spending time with God, or that God's just spoken to them and wonder what it's actually like for that person, how it happens.

Do you think of all the "I can't's"? "I can't hear from God like that." "I don't know how to spend time with God." "I don't know how to be a companion to Jesus." "I can't see how I can fit it all into my busy, busy life."

An idea has got around that developing this relationship with Jesus is the hardest, most complicated thing to achieve, even that it's only possible for some super spiritual people. But, if you really think about that idea, you realise that it must have been circulated by the devil. We have been made by God for intimacy with God, made to be Jesus' companion, made to walk with an awareness of the Holy Spirit with us. This is the most natural thing for us to be able to do. There can surely be nothing easier to obtain than the enjoyment of this relationship because Jesus' desire to give Himself, and to know us, is far greater than ours to receive and know Him.

So first of all, I want to encourage you to relax about it! Whoever you are, whatever you've done, it's time to expect to have a great relationship with Jesus. Expect to get to know Him and love Him. Expect to hear His voice. **Expect that this is going to be the best thing in your life, the thing that gives your life meaning and purpose and the thing that makes you the woman you were made to be.** So lose all the "I can't's" that you've allowed yourself to be controlled by and start to say: "I can!" and believe it!

The next few chapters will help you with the "I can't's" by giving you some 'HOW TO'. They're not a definitive guide to having a relationship with God but hopefully will inspire and encourage you to see that you don't actually need a relationship manual because this is about you and Him being together in your own unique way. It may have been made to seem complicated and religious but really this relationship with Jesus can be summed up in three simple little words:

PERSON TO PERSON

A Person To Person Relationship

As Jesus and His disciples continued on their way to Jerusalem, they came to a village where a woman named Martha welcomed them into her home. Her sister, Mary, sat at the Lord's feet, listening to what He taught. But Martha was worrying over the big dinner she was preparing. She came to Jesus and said, "Lord, doesn't it seem unfair to you that my sister just sits here while I do all the work? Tell her to come and help me."

*But the Lord said to her, "My dear Martha, you are so upset over all these details! There is really only **one thing** worth being concerned about. Mary has discovered it – and I won't take it away from her."*
(Luke 10:38-42 NLT)

What was the 'one thing' that this woman had found? **Friendship, relationship, intimacy with Jesus.** Mary got the whole relationship thing in a way that her sister didn't. For Mary, it was simply **person to person**.

And this is the only way our relationship with God will work. We can read books, hear sermons and learn about Jesus, but knowing *about* someone is completely different to knowing them. Or, we can be introduced to God and find that we relate to Him as a helper and provider – we seek Him for our needs. It's not that we shouldn't do that but when it's *all* we do, it prevents a close relationship!

My point exactly

When we seek Him instead as a *person* and receive Him for who He is, not just for what He can do; and when we freely give ourselves, for Him to receive and enjoy us as a *person* – just for who we are, we find all we have been longing for our whole lives.

This relationship is our **invitation to life**. Jesus expresses it best when He requests the pleasure of YOUR company:

INVITATION

Are you tired? Worn out? Burnt out on religion?
COME TO ME.
Get away with me and you'll recover your life.
I'll show you how to take a real rest.
Walk with me and work with me – *watch how I do it.*
Learn the unforced rhythms of grace.
I won't lay anything heavy or ill-fitting on you.
Keep company with me and you'll learn to live freely and lightly.
(Matthew 11 MSG)

JESUS:

Of Nazareth (Acts 22:8), Carpenter's Son (Matt 13:55), Son of God (Rom 1:4), Alpha & Omega (Rev 21:6), Saviour of the World (1Jn 4:14), Almighty (Rev 1:8), Deliverer (Rom 11:26), King of Kings (Rev 17:14), Bread of Life (Jn 6:35), Most Mighty (Ps 45:3), Judge (Mic 5:1), Prince of Peace (Is 9:6), Power of God (1Cor 1:24), Faithful & True (Rev 19:11), Good Shepherd (Jn 10:11), Head over all things (Eph 1:22), Wonderful (Is 9:6), Image of the Invisible God (Col 1:15), God with us (Mt 1:23), WAY, TRUTH, LIFE (Jn 14:16), Life in abundance, to the full, till it overflows (Jn 10:10), Word of God (1Jn 1:1), Eternal Life (1 Jn 5:20), Messiah (Dan 9:25), Friend (Jn 15:15)

11

THE HOW TO: Changing Your Attitude To Love

As God's daughters, we can enjoy a relationship with the perfect **parent**. We can have a lot of fun with the best of **friends** – the one who sticks closer than a sibling (Proverbs 18:24). There is no kind of love left out with God. No part of our hearts overlooked. In the Bible, He says that He is our **husband** (Isaiah 54:5, Hosea 2) and Jesus is our **bridegroom** and we are His bride (Revelation18:23). Your desire to be loved and cherished is God's very own desire for you.

Damaged Lovers

But in order to have true intimacy with God, to really know Him fully in all these ways, we need to put off all the lessons about relationships that we've been taught by this fallen world. When you hear that God is your FATHER, that He is your HUSBAND, your FRIEND, your TEACHER, do you have reservations because of earthly relationships you've experienced? Think about the negative things you think about love. Perhaps you've thought some of the following or have other things to add to the list:

☐   Love means having to change/ compromise who I really am to attract anyone.

☐   Love can never be as good for me as it is for other people. They're more attractive and more lovable than me so they must be able to have a much more satisfying love relationship than I ever could.

☐   Love can never really be true and perfect anyway.

☐   Love is not and may never be part of my experience.

☐   Love means being abused, hurt, used.

☐   Love means always feeling insecure in the other person's affection.

☐   Love means a lifetime of fearing rejection and struggling to keep the person's love.

☐   Love's the best feeling in the world – better than... God. God's good for people who can't get real human love. He makes up for what they're missing.

☐

☐

Perfect Love

All the disappointments, and the defences we've put up in relationships, have stopped us realising true love is real and possible, that it is attentive, devoted, passionate, perfect. Because Jesus' love is simply not something we can compare with love as we know it in our fallen world. He is never distracted but always intensely interested. He understands you completely and doesn't make fun of you. He likes you! He actually wants the best for you. He cares about you. He doesn't pull you down to make Himself look good. He doesn't laugh at you and mock you. He makes you feel of infinite value – never cheap.

He enjoys the way you are – your laughter, the way you think, your voice, your singing, all your funniest little ways – everything – and is never bored by it. He thinks you're amazing and not ordinary and He'll be your friend when no one else will. He doesn't rush ahead and leave you panting to keep up. He doesn't fall asleep on you – ever. He picks you for his team straight away. He always wants to pair up with you. There's a seat permanently saved beside Him with your name on it. He asks you to dance every single time.

He never holds back and He never manipulates or throws a tantrum. He doesn't stand you up or let you down. He keeps promises always. He's available 24/7. You can't come on too strong, you can't be too weak or feeble, you can't leave Him unsatisfied and looking for anything better. He doesn't start a fight and He doesn't argue. You can't do anything He isn't willing to forgive. His eye never even glances elsewhere. His feelings for you never waver. **You can only be certain of His love.**

God is not like people. He isn't a bad father, an absent, disinterested father or even a 'good' father. He is a Perfect Father. Perfect Husband. Perfect Teacher. Perfect Friend. His love is immeasurable. **It is perfect love.** He could not love you with a greater love. And He doesn't love anybody else more than you, EVEN JESUS (John 15:9, 17:22). It isn't less than love between two human lovers – it is more than earthly love could ever be. Perfect love really is forever. Perfect love can satisfy the great desire of your life to be known and longed for, the fulfilment of all you could ever have dreamt of. Perfect love is true contentment because the great cry of the human heart is met.

Life may have convinced you perfect love doesn't exist but take some time now to let your imagination run wild and think what the love affair you dream of, the romances you long to be part of – real intimacy with perfect love – could look like in your life.

RECEIVING PERFECT LOVE – BEING WITH SOMEONE WHO:
- [ ] Desires and appreciates you.
- [ ] Likes the way you look.
- [ ] You are so in love with, you know you'll never get bored.
- [ ] You can rely on to carry you through everything – wherever you go He'll hold your hand, put His arm around you, not let you go for a second.
- [ ] Is so absorbed in you all the time that you never have to feel at all nervous but have peace and rest.
- [ ] You can do things with that are a bit daring because you're safe in His arms.
- [ ] Makes everything fun and enjoyable.
- [ ] You know has made sound plans and will take care of anything the future throws up so you can look forward to everything.
- [ ]
- [ ]

GIVING YOUR LOVE – YOU BEING SOMEONE WHO:
- [ ] Provides pleasure.
- [ ] Lets Him know that you appreciate Him and His strength.
- [ ] Lets Him know that you're 100% His.
- [ ] Makes things nice for Him – a nice place for Him to live, little ways of entertaining Him, making things fun.

☐   Does all you can to assist Him in being all He can be and achieving all He wants to.

☐   Cheers Him on in public and in private.

☐

☐

Girls Romanced

The ways God does love are various and always inventive. It may be His voice deep in your spirit, a Bible verse or passage that comes alive to you, a gift of flowers at just the right moment, a kind word from a stranger or a friend, a slogan on an advert even, or something in nature which God uses to speak through like an arrow piercing the bulls eye of your heart.

Here is a glimpse of God's Perfect Love in a handful of women's lives:

★ ★ ★

'"How's your love life?" There have been times when I've been quick to answer, "I don't have one." But lately my answer has changed. I... now find myself answering with a smile on my face, "It is just simply divine."

Divine indeed! Because my love interest is not just any man... Yes, you guessed it; the lover of my soul is Jesus. We've got a love thing going on!'

As Michelle McKinney Hammond's friends asked her how she had fallen in love with Jesus, she thought about it and realised that it had happened through her looking for God in everything – 'good or bad', she 'tracked Him down in the middle of it'. She likens it to when tourists go to Hollywood and keep trying to spot the rich and famous and eventually they do see someone. She says:

'I believe we have to look for God in that very way. And when we seek Him, we find Him'.

– Michelle McKinney Hammond[39]

★ ★ ★

Stasi Eldredge says: 'Every song you love, every memory you cherish, every moment that has moved you to holy tears has been given to you from the One who has been pursuing you from your first breath in order to win your heart...

We have missed many of His notes simply because we shut our hearts down in order to endure the pain of life... we must open our hearts again, and keep them open'.

She describes how her husband, John, was on a business trip and went down to the beach to pray. Sitting in the sand, watching the waves, he saw a massive humpback whale 'impossibly close to shore'. He knew that this was a gift to his heart from God.

Stasi wanted to be overwhelmed by God's love for her in the same way and when she was sitting, looking out to sea, she asked Jesus that if He loved her like He loved John, could she have a whale too. Nothing happened so she got up and started to walk. She describes rounding a corner and seeing a starfish. The whale had been especially for John but this was **God's kiss for her**. She thanked Him for it and rounded another bend. She describes the sight that met her:

'Before me, behind me, surrounding me, were hundreds of starfish. Zillions of them... God didn't just love me. He LOOOOVED me! Intimately, personally, completely'.

– Stasi Eldredge[40]

★ ★ ★

Joyce Meyer says: 'One day as I was driving down the road, God spoke to my heart and said, "Joyce, you're the apple of My eye."'

God then showed her a picture of a lady in a supermarket looking through a pile of apples to find the best one. Joyce felt that God was telling her that she was the best 'apple' to Him!

She says: 'At first I didn't receive what He was saying because I felt condemned for thinking such nice things about myself'.

What she didn't know was that He was actually speaking to her from the Bible which she discovered a couple of days later when she opened her Bible on Psalm 17:8: *Keep me as the apple of your eye* (NIV). What God had been saying became real to her and blessed her by making her feel special for a long time afterwards.

She goes on to say: 'I remember a time when the Lord ministered to me and said, "Joyce, I do so many things for people every day because I love them, and they don't even see it." Then He gave me this example: "Every day when I speak to the sun and say, "Rise," I do it for you."'

– Joyce Meyer[41]

★ ★ ★

God's voice comes in so many different forms. One day I was waiting to be served in a shop. I was feeling under a lot of pressure and I became very aware of the tune playing. It was a song with what could have been an annoyingly repetitive lyric but I knew that this wasn't just some boy singing a love song about him and a girl. In that moment, this was God's voice publicly singing love songs about Him and me, that:

"Together we're invincible."

That really lodged in my heart and helped me through the rest of the day and on occasions since then. God is so inventive and fun in the ways He has to touch our hearts. I just wonder how many times I've missed kisses from Him and know that I don't want to anymore

– Anna Symonds

★ ★ ★

In *My Single Mom Life*, Angela Thomas writes about speaking at a conference on Valentine's Day and telling the women that God calls them beautiful. But inside her there was a lonely emptiness – no flowers, no chocolates, no calls or text messages had come her way. At the airport that evening, soaking wet from heavy rain, she says: "I moped toward my gate, feeling as unloved and unnoticed as a woman could feel." She spots one of the most handsome men she has ever seen. He touches her sleeve and says: "You are vaary beau-tee-full" in a thick Italian accent. She describes it:

"My eyes instantly filled with tears, because I knew what had just happened. If that man had said anything else to me, it wouldn't have meant what it meant that day. I knew God Himself had just walked across Concourse B. He had spoken to me the very words I had said to the other women all weekend. *You're beautiful.*

I almost began weeping aloud, doubled over from the sweetness of it all."

– Angela Thomas[42]

★ ★ ★

How about you? Do you desire that 'one thing' Mary had that nothing could surpass? That person to person relationship that gives you reason for being. Then tell God – it's His desire for you, that you would let Him love you and allow Jesus to show you perfect love.

In the next three chapters, still looking at HOW TO have a really great relationship with Jesus, we're going to consider three particular ways that God's perfect love differs from love in this fallen world and how we need to choose this love that satisfies, this love that you can trust and this love that desires the real you.

12

THE HOW TO: Choosing The Love That Satisfies

The 'Real Deal'

> The whole universe was in that look. Everything. The past, the future, the sun, the sky, every pair of shoes Marc Jacobs ever designed, every Bellini, every ball gown, every trip to Rio I'd ever taken (=sex)... He's the REAL DEAL. Kind, adorable, the cutest thing ever.
>
> *– Bergdorf Blondes*[43]

This is the moment that the heroine in this novel realises that the hero is *her* hero – something better than the very best of the best things in her life: he's the 'real deal'.

Isn't the 'real deal' what all mankind is looking for? That person, place or thing out there, where we'll find the ultimate eureka moment, the something that would be better than the best of the best? The world has us searching in all kinds of directions, promising we'll find this elusive something, that will give us satisfaction, in earth shattering success in our work, in travel and adventure, in drugs or alcohol, in money, in having children, in plastic surgery, in pursuing learning or in things we can buy like a new house or even clothes. But more than anywhere, this fallen world tells us that we will find it in love – if we can find the perfect man that is!

Most girls grow up longing for an experience like the heroine's in *Bergdorf Blondes*. It's partly the way we're made to be. God's design for many men and women is for them to live in couples and raise children. And where that partnership is part of people's lives, God intends for it to be wonderful, but not for it to be *enough* for any one of us.

The deep yearning in us is for even more than romantic human love can ever give because we were made by God for God and we will never be whole apart from Him. That 'real deal' we long for will not be found without His presence in our lives. That's not just a bit, or even a lot, of Christian activity, theological study or church involvement – it's the intimate, personal relationship that takes us beyond spirituality and religion to really falling in love, to an exchange of affection, to mutual pleasure, to a living, breathing, eternal love affair.

The problem can be that when we do discover God, we continue to search for satisfaction outside of Him. We find ourselves behaving a bit like:

The Unfaithful Wife

This woman makes God really sad. He addresses her in Jeremiah 2, Hosea 2 and Ezekiel 16, calling her a rebel, a harlot, a whore, an adulterous wife. In spite of all He's done for her:

*   She calls to God only when she needs help – the rest of the time she forgets all about Him and what He's done for her.
*   She feels the freedom that comes from having her shame removed and uses the beauty she now has to find pleasure and fulfilment outside of God – making herself available to other lovers.
*   She doesn't appreciate that all she has are gifts from His hand and takes what He has given to her to make shrines for her idols.
*   Gaining acceptance and adoration from the world is still her main goal. She is probably saying: "I can't love me until the world loves me", not: "I'll love me because God does."

The Fear Of Missing Out

Although this woman's behaviour sounds awful, you may know something of what it's like to feel that you haven't found all you're looking for in God.

The 'real deal' still seems to elude you. You're still dissatisfied and unhappy. A part of you is still looking for something better.

You may be saying: "If God's meant to be enough, the 'real deal', meet my needs, then why do I still want so much more? Like position, wealth, success, family's approval, friends' acceptance or perfect love with a MAN? Why do I still have to find my identity in what people think, in what I do, in who my partner is?"

That's how I used to be. I loved God, I knew He loved me but when I looked at my circumstances, the way life seemed to be turning out, God didn't seem to be enough. When I was flicking through *Bergdorf Blondes*, that paragraph that's above jumped off the page. At the start of that year, I'd heard a sermon where we were encouraged to leave behind the bad things of the previous 12 months and move forward into the new year. The speaker said something like: "Tell the Lord what you've had enough of, what you want for this year…" And rather than the lengthy prayer which I might have imagined I would pray, of all the things I wanted to be rid of and become, the cry of my heart was five words:

"I WANT THE REAL DEAL"

I'm not sure I knew what I was asking for except that I'd had enough of a life that wasn't it. If nothing could surpass a relationship with God and He really was THE ULTIMATE, BEST OF THE BEST OF THE BEST then I didn't want to stop short of really experiencing it. I got my miracle that year – I found the 'real deal' relationship with Jesus that's been everything to me ever since. There have been no more days feeling dissatisfied! And that's the relationship you can have with Him too!

I think that there are a couple of important factors involved:

1. Losing The Regret And Suspicion

I read about Darlene Zschech's father – a man who had definitely found the 'real deal' in his relationship with God. She talks about her distress when he was very ill with cancer and wasn't being healed in spite of many prayers. She felt he really needed a miracle but he said:

"I already have my miracle, **I know Jesus**; I have salvation, and that is enough – **that is enough for me**."

Her father 'saw that Jesus is the greatest miracle of all'. He 'didn't need a healing miracle to feel fulfilled; his friendship with Jesus was the fulfilment of his life's purpose'.[44]

That really challenged and inspired me. I wanted to be able to say the same thing – that Jesus was my more than enough. I mentioned it to someone who was passionate in her pursuit of God but rather than encourage me, she said: "Wow! That's really brave." What she was actually saying was that she'd rather me than her – it was just a bit too fanatical, a bit too desperate. And that's so much of our problem. There is a sense that if we choose to discover God as the 'real deal' then we'll a) be missing out and b) probably be letting ourselves in for a lot of trouble.

We're aware that choosing a life with God is about commitment and dedication to Him. Most people who choose to follow Jesus have heard His words to His disciples:

> *"If anyone desires to be My disciple, let him deny himself **[disregard, lose sight of, and forget himself and his own interests]** and take up his cross and follow Me [cleave steadfastly to Me, conform wholly to My example in living and, if need be, in dying, also]."*
> (Matthew 16:24 AMP)

And their flesh has risen up. They wonder if taking up their cross and following Jesus is going to make them miss out on too many good things. The devil certainly helps us to think so. He wants us to fear that the price is too big of choosing dedication to God. He tells us that living life God's way is like choosing a prison, losing our freedom. We feel deprived and resentful, thinking: "I can't", "I must", "I've got to," "I never will again," "I'm not allowed" all the time. He draws our eyes to the 'fun' everyone else is having, tricking us into thinking that **we've got God but we've still got to go on searching for the 'real deal' life.**

I had decided on dedication to God, but so deep down, it was almost subconsciously, I regretted that He was *all* I'd chosen. There were other voices I wanted to listen to too, and other enjoyments that I wished that I could have as well, that I had abandoned.

God really uncovered the exact way I felt when He told me that He wanted me to be "satisfied" by Him but that my reaction was: "to think that's like living on gruel." It was so true. I believed God *could* 'satisfy' me. Like good solid porridge, He wouldn't leave me hungry. But yuck! How boring! How unvaried! How uncolourful, unflavoursome! How unenjoyable!

But God said: **"I am every kind of food and drink – you can never be bored of me."**

After that, verses kept popping up to confirm what God had said like:

> *In Your presence is fullness of joy, at Your right hand there are pleasures forevermore.*
> (Psalm 16:11 AMP)

> *"Open your mouth wide, and I will fill it with good things."*
> (Psalm 81:10 NLT)

> *They relish and feast on the abundance of Your house; and You cause them to drink of the stream of Your pleasures.*
> (Psalm 36:8 AMP)

God wanted me to stop the self pity and see instead of Him being 'all' I'd chosen as something small and lacking that it was 'all' meaning EVERYTHING. We can well afford to make God our all and sacrifice everything else because this isn't some grey old gruel we're being offered but the richest of fare, the most varied, eternal banquet.

God has never taken away our free will. You need to remind yourself that you don't *have* to live God's way but you're *choosing* to because you want to, because you love Him and because it doesn't get any better than what He offers.

You can lose the regret because you won't be missing out and you can lose the suspicion too because you aren't letting yourself in for a lot of trouble. God is good, not some harsh task-master looking to harm, hurt or destroy you. He desires to look after you, bless you, to share your life with you, that you would laugh together with Him and receive His love.

God wants you free, whole, healed, stable and strong. He wants an end to all the hurt, the pain, the hiding in shame, the years that have been stolen so that you can properly **BECOME** _Rachael_ and He can

(insert your name here)

use you, direct you, see you step into the fullness of your future, fruitful and fulfilled.

2. Always Reaching For More!

"So, what's the future?" I asked Jesus, on one occasion, and He said: "ME". In the past I would have seen that as pretty terrifying. A future of other people having a good time and poor hard done by me having God. But now I know God is all the money, career, husbands, children, homes, travel, success, adventure, happiness, thrills and excitement the future may provide, that there is nothing better. Nothing is going to start that's better. Nothing is going to happen that's better. That is no compromise, no lack, no shortfall. That's the 'real deal'. That is truly blessed.

The Amplified Bible amplifies the word 'blessed':

> Blessed (happy with life-joy and **satisfaction in God's favour and salvation, apart from your outward condition** - and to be envied).
>
> (Luke 6:21 AMP)

When we stop regretting our choice, a whole world of living blessed begins to open up to us, not relying on an old experience of being satisfied, but a continuous outpouring as we press in to know God more and more. We should ever be asking for the boundaries in revelation and relationship to be pushed out. There is always more Jesus – that's the abundance (John 10:10 AMP). What we have begun is a life long pursuit, an exploration into the infinite riches and wonders of the Father, Son and Spirit.

Even when we know the wonder of having a relationship with God, there remains within us a desire for more which is a good thing that we shouldn't feel bad about. We can be desperate for more, yearning with all our heart's desire, but instead of taking that desire to other lovers, directing it towards God. We should find our satisfaction in Jesus but continue to reach for more of Him:

> *Seek, inquire of and for the Lord, and* **crave Him** *and His strength (His might and inflexibility to temptation); seek and require His face and His presence [continually] evermore.*
> (Psalm 105:4 AMP)

C.S.Lewis says that we are inclined to stop short of enjoying all that God offers because we think that to desire 'our own good and earnestly to hope for the enjoyment of it is a bad thing' but that feeling hasn't come from God:

> 'If we consider… the staggering nature of the rewards promised in the Gospels, it would seem that Our Lord finds our desires, not too strong, but too weak. We are half-hearted creatures, fooling about with drink and sex and ambition when infinite joy is offered us, like an ignorant child who wants to go on making mud pies in a slum because he cannot imagine what is meant by the offer of a holiday at the sea. We are far too easily pleased'.
>
> —C.S. Lewis[45]

Your 'Real Deal'

What's the 'real deal' to you? The dream that would be better than the best of the best? What are you so desperate for you feel if you don't get it/them you can't possibly know fullness of life? Could your desires be drawing you to God and the life He wants for you, that Jesus has died to make available. Could it be that the desire behind all your desire is that longing for the 'real deal' that is a relationship with Him?

Have you searched for the 'real deal' but been left empty, unable to find anything you can do for yourself, or get from anywhere else, that actually sustains you and makes you whole? Where, if ever, have you come close to finding that unsurpassable eureka moment? Do you think it's possible to find the 'real deal' in God?

In a relationship. You are taught a little of God's love through the love for and of a man. Although, nothing surpasses the feeling of being so on fire for God. You can definitely find the 'real deal' in God. And I want to.

So ask Him that whatever circumstances you're in, you would be able to enjoy His presence with you and replace your cravings – for a different body, more money, greater success or a man or friends to be God to you – with a deep contentment. That's not a righteous compromise – picking contentment God's way because it seems like the right or worthy thing and then somehow missing out. This is a contentment that is unsurpassable. This is about being truly satisfied in a way you could never have believed would be possible because you have discovered the worship we were made for and the only One worthy of our complete devotion. This has got to be better than absolutely anything in existence. So ask for it. Be unwilling to settle for anything less than the 'real deal'.

Thank you Jesus.

13

THE HOW TO: Choosing The Love You Can Trust

Whenever things got a little bit tricky, my Grandmother's solution was always the same. She'd say: "You just need a man for that." She wasn't young, she'd been married and had two sons. It wasn't that she hadn't had her own significant achievements and interests because she had, but she was used to getting a little bit of help from 'the boys' when there was a need for physical strength, a big decision to be made or a financial matter to sort out.

Now we're used to aspiring to be superwomen – there's hardly an area of life where women don't excel and we've proven that we actually don't 'need' a man in order to do anything we want to. But sometimes that has left us pursuing independence in our relationship with God. We can find ourselves acting a bit like we're Jesus' elder sister or feel we should be. We have such a sense of responsibility that it wears us out – responsibility for life, others, to God, to ourselves, to the world. We try to fight the battles in our lives with our own strength and with our own bare hands. We even start fighting other people's for them.

The devil wants us worn out from living like this. But it's not how we have to be. We're not fatherless. We're not on our own to try desperately to be brave and strong. God has the strategy to give us the victory in every circumstance. **So we can actually rest in being God's child (Matthew 18:4), the girl who doesn't feel like a capable grown up, the vulnerable wife who wants a husband she can lean and depend on.**

God Alone Will *Always* Come Through For Us

We don't have to depend on other humans and have extreme expectations of them which is just as well. However well meaning they may be, there is nobody we can rely on to come through for us every time. Even a devoted husband, parent or friend, who desires to do just that, may be unable to achieve it. That's left most of us afraid – maybe not consciously frightened all the time, but uneasy deep inside – about what may happen.

When we look at some of the circumstances in our lives, we can feel very anxious which is just what the devil wants – to bind us up with fear. Fear is a spirit, not just an emotional response, and it torments our minds if we allow it to. But it isn't the spirit God has given to us. We have the Holy Spirit – the spirit of a 'sound mind' (2Timothy 1:7 NKJV). Our minds don't have to be full of fearful thoughts.

But we won't combat fear just by deciding not to worry, being positive, or putting mind over matter, feeling we should be self-confident women and struggling to act like we are.

No, the only way we can combat fear is if our minds are filled instead with thoughts of God's love and goodness. The Bible is absolutely full of the assurance that God loves us and will come through for us every single moment of every single day. And this is the key to swapping fear for faith – a solid, unshakeable belief that what God says is true. It is a certain hope based on God and what He says in the Bible.

The more we know we are loved and that God desires to be good to us, the more readily we will reject the fearful thoughts the devil tries to introduce into our minds. God loved us when we were far from Him, when we never gave Him a thought and were doing our worst. He loved us, not because we did good things, but in our most completely fallen state. He chose to lay down His life – His desire for companionship with us was so great. Now that we have chosen to receive what Jesus has done for us and become His companions, why would He suddenly abandon us?

It takes a big change in the way we think to begin to live believing that there is someone who will *always* come through for us. But what a wonderful difference it makes to life. If you allow the love of God to consume you, the truth about His goodness, you can live with confidence – not in other people or in yourself – but in HIM. Then:

THERE IS **NOTHING** TO BE AFRAID OF EVER AGAIN!

Always, Always, Always Good

If you really believe God will never harm you, you can live surrendered to His love instead of surrendered to fear. Fear has to be replaced with an insistence on the truth. God is good ALL THE TIME. He is thinking good, loving, kind thoughts towards you ALL THE TIME, *innumerable, precious* thoughts for your welfare, benefit, blessing and peace (Psalm 139:17-18 NLT, Jeremiah 29:11). You're never off His mind. He never, ever forgets about you. He pays close and careful attention. He is *on your side and takes your part* (Psalm 118:7 AMP). You can have *perfect and constant peace* if your mind is immovably focused on God (Isaiah 26:3 AMP).

A few years ago, I had no concept of God thinking anything nice about me and I remember being really struck when I heard this worship song and thought that God could actually be smiling at *me*!:

> As my love for You grows strong
> Close to You is where I long to be
> As I gaze into Your eyes
> Such a look of pure delight I see
> **Lord You're smiling at me**
> > – Nigel Hemming[46]

We need to continuously be ready to confess God's goodness and praise Him for it. We have to remain at all times of the opinion that God is good. We have to say that He is good whatever happens and thank Him for it. We have to praise His name at every turn. We have to meditate on this FACT – fill our minds with the truth – that God is:

Good all the time!

Give thanks to the Lord, for He is good.   *Praise the Lord, for the Lord is good.*

(Psalm1136:1 NLT)   (Psalm 135:3 NLT)

Even in the hardest times, the situations where God's promise is as yet unfulfilled or a problem seems to take forever to be resolved, we can still declare the truth that God is good. He wants to do us good, and only good. That He is doing good on our behalf and will work all things out for good. It's very easy to doubt God at those times but we must choose to continue to pursue companionship with our loving Father rather than sinking in fears. Keep delighting to: **'Give God your warmest smile!'** (Psalm 34:5, MSG).

As we pursue God, opening our loving, trusting hearts to Him, allowing His Spirit to pray through us, we can rest assured:

> *The Spirit pleads for us believers in harmony with God's own will. And we know that **God causes everything to work together for the good of those who love God** and are called according to his purpose for them.*
>
> (Romans 8:27-28 NLT)

David said that he didn't know what would have become of him if he hadn't believed that he would see *the goodness of the Lord in the land of the living* (Psalm 27:13 AMP). He goes on to say: *Wait and hope for and expect the Lord; be brave and of good courage and let your heart be stout and enduring. Yes, wait for and hope for and expect the Lord.* (Psalm 27:14 AMP)

What will happen to us if we don't make this our lifestyle? David knew for him that it would have meant something pretty terrible. We need to believe we will see God's goodness every day in the ordinary activities of life. No matter what we're going through we have to put hope in His goodness and expect Him to move in the situations we face. We need to expect that something good is going to happen to us. We have to become women of hope – women who have a:

CONFIDENT EXPECTATION OF GOD'S GOODNESS

Women who can wake up, go to bed and move through each day and say like David did:

> *Surely or only* **GOODNESS**, *mercy, and unfailing love shall follow me all the days of my life.*
> (Psalm 23:6 AMP)

Careless In The Care Of God (Matthew 6:26 MSG)

The Bible tells us how we should deal with the troubles of life – the stresses, strains, anxieties, worries, irritations, negative feelings, frustrations, insults – all our cares in fact. The advice is quite simply to hand them over to God:

> *Cast your cares on the Lord and He will sustain you.*
> (Psalm 55:22 NIV)

> *Don't worry about anything; instead, pray about everything. Tell God what you need, and thank Him for all He has done. If you do this, you will experience God's peace, which is far more wonderful than the human mind can understand. His peace will guard your hearts and minds as you live in Christ Jesus.*
> (Philippians 4:6-7 NLT)

That's not praying and then fretting but praying and relaxing because you know God will take care of you and your circumstances. You don't know when or how He will meet your needs but it doesn't matter because you know that He definitely will.

Get ready to be treated like the heroine who is so valuable her God will never ever forsake her, let her down or harm her. God is longing to be good to you, looking for you to expect His goodness, to be looking out for it all the time, eagerly trusting Him and anticipating demonstrations of His love:

> *The Lord [earnestly] waits [expecting, looking, and longing] to be gracious to you; and therefore He lifts Himself up, that He may have mercy on you and show loving-kindness to you. For the Lord is a God of justice. Blessed (happy, fortunate, to be envied) are all those who [earnestly] wait for Him, who expect and look and long for Him [for His victory, His favour, His love, his peace, His joy, and His*

matchless, unbroken companionship]!
(Isaiah 30:18 AMP)

Jehoshaphat was a man who found himself surrounded by enemies and he felt afraid but instead of giving in to the fear, he *set himself [determinedly, as his vital need] to seek the Lord* (2Chronicles 20:3 AMP). He had a big challenge, some very difficult circumstances that he was up against, so He looked to God to be good to Him, to provide a strategy and give him a way to take the victory.

His prayer gives us a helpful example of how we can avoid becoming battle weary. He begins by establishing the throne, glory and power of God – *"In Your hand are power and might, so that none is able to withstand You"* (2Chronicles 20:6 AMP).   He establishes the word of God – speaking the promises God has already made. Then he speaks to God about the situation, He lays it before God and asks for help. He says that they don't know what to do about it but they know God does. And God directs them to take the victory.

Speak It Out

You know how important your words are. Psalm 91 is full of promises of God's protection – from evil plots, diseases and death – for the person who has set their love on Him (v.14), has made God their *dwelling place* (v.1, v.9), the person who will:

> *'SAY of the Lord, He is my Refuge and my Fortress, my God; on Him I lean and rely, and in Him I [confidently] trust!'*
> (Psalm 91:2 AMP)

You need to speak aloud the truth, those positive words that express your growing hope – that confident expectation of His goodness:

"You are being good to me. You do and will take care of me. I will lack no good thing. I love God and life. I am blessed. *I am more than a conqueror* (Romans 8:37 AMP). *I have victory wherever I go* (2Samuel 8:6 AMP). *You go before me. You march with me; You will not fail me or let me go or forsake me* (Deuteronomy 31:8 AMP).

Focus on this promise that at all times, in all things, you will have *all* that you need:

> *God is able to make all grace, every favour, and earthly blessing, come to me **in abundance** so I may always, under all circumstances, whatever the need, be self-sufficient.*
>
> (2 Corinthians 9:8 AMP).

I am going to have an amazing day/ week/ year/ life in Jesus' name. By Your grace, I will break through every obstacle, scale every wall, defeat every enemy and bring down every giant. I am going to fulfill Your purposes for me. You know what the future holds. You have a plan for me. It is good. And by your power, I will fulfill it in Jesus' name."

That's Beautiful

A woman who radiates her true loveliness, who allows the beauty God has bestowed upon her to be displayed? A woman who trusts God. A woman who is peaceful because she lives like God is good.

> *You should be known for the beauty that comes from within, the unfading beauty of a gentle and quiet spirit, which is so precious to God. That is the way the holy women of old made themselves beautiful.* **They trusted God.**
>
> (1Peter 3:4–5 NLT)

14

THE HOW TO: Choosing The Love That Desires The Real You

Our experiences of relationships in this fallen world leave us feeling that we can't be acceptable to another person the way we are. This makes us imagine the same goes for God – that we have got to do things to make Him love us. We lose sight of the fact that we are acceptable to Him because Jesus has replaced our shameful, sinful nature with His glory. It can make us what I think of as a 'Textbook Wife' to God.

The Textbook Wife

- On the outside, this is the kind of woman who looks like the perfect Christian but she's actually a legalistic, programmed robot (or Stepford wife![47] – a Pharisee[48] in Jesus' day).
- She's like someone who's read every relationship manual and follows the instructions to the letter to attract and keep the object of her affection.
- She doesn't know that she's truly accepted by God so she abides by rules and regulations to earn His approval.
- She is trying so hard to be good, she can become self-righteous seeing other people's sin and thinking that they deserve God's punishment. Do you know the parable of the prodigal son in Luke 15? She is rather like his elder brother.[49]

A Christian Version Of Myself

I don't know about you but I have certainly had attributes of the Textbook

Wife at times – trying to be some Christian version of myself with God! A model of perfection, rather than someone desperately in need of God in the reality of her humanity. It seems crazy but I could spend time praying and never tell God about the deepest concerns I had. It was a bit like posting my prayers as letters, pushing them into the post box instead of sitting with God face to face.

Deep down, I had so much pent up emotion I ignored to share with God. I was sort of keeping it secret but it weighed on my mind. Many of my desires, hurts, griefs, longings, disappointments and fears were guiltily suppressed. I'd never told Him the honest truth about certain things that really embarrassed me and I felt guilty about.

There were times I plain forgot about God – there was something I needed to work out so I would – without giving Him a thought.

I knew that God wanted my faith so I'd pray sentences that sounded faith filled, like: "Lord, your word says that you will protect your children, X is your daughter. Thank you that you are going before her on that journey and will look after her and keep her safe." Then I would be frantic with worry that X was going to be in a terrible accident. Or I'd ask for direction: "Lord, you promise to guide me, thank you that I *will* know what to do." And then I'd try to work it all out for myself and I wouldn't have a clue what decisions to make. I'd be so stressed I wouldn't even be listening for God's answer.

People hurt me and I'd think about it and cry but I'd avoid going over it with God. I kept my feelings to myself, spending ages turning them over in my head or talking them over with someone else but I was too ashamed to take them to God. In the end, of course, all that mess inside just leads to bitterness and anger and misery. You stew in your own juices and dry out as a person:

> *When I kept it all inside,*
> *my bones turned to powder,*
> *my words became daylong groans.*

> *The pressure never let up;*

all the juices of my life dried up.

Then I let it all out;
I said, "I'll make a clean breast of my failures to God."

Suddenly the pressure was gone –
my guilt dissolved,
my sin disappeared.

(Psalm 32 MSG)

If I couldn't be really open with God, really me, then what was the point? IT WASN'T LIKE HE DIDN'T KNOW IT ALL ANYWAY! Trying to present to God as perfect was living a lie and stopping me being me. It stunted our relationship and God began to show me that. I could see that He would prefer to hear my honest pleas than all that piety. I really believe it's like praise when we pour our hearts out to God. We value human relationships where we feel trusted and confided in. How much God must like it when we feel that we can talk to Him in a way we can't to anyone else, that He's that special to us!

You're The One That He Wants!

The Textbook Wife doesn't feel free to be herself with God. But that is exactly what God desires us to be. Never think that your relationship with God doesn't matter, that you're dispensable or He prefers the love He has with someone else. You can think you're just one person over the whole of history – just you – nothing special. But you're unique and God's love for you is just for you. He can't have what He desires with you with anybody else.

Jesus is saying about you:

"my dove, my perfect one, is UNIQUE."

(Song of Solomon 6:9 NIV)

There's no one like her on earth,
never has been, never will be.

(Song of Solomon 6:8 MSG)

It really matters to Him that He receives real love from the real you. It can be easier to hold back your truest self because you've learnt to give other people what you think will make them like you. You may have felt that you've needed to withdraw in relationships because people won't approve, that the kindest thing you can do is stay away altogether or hide parts of yourself. It may have been hard to imagine anyone enjoying anything about you. But God wants you to be real with Him, not a Christian version of yourself. **Only you can be you and do all God has planned for you to do. Only you can have the relationship with Him that He *desires* from you!**

Hear it in His own words – He desires that you would look at Him and say something:

> *"Let me see you; let me hear your voice. For your voice is pleasant and you are lovely."*
> (Song of Songs 2:14 NLT)

It takes your love to conquer His heart:

> *"You have ravished my heart, my treasure, my bride. I am overcome by one glance of your eyes, by a single bead of your necklace."*
> (Song of Solomon 4:9 NLT)

You truly are a source of pleasure. Jesus even likes the taste and smell of you. Your kisses are delightful to Him:

> *"Your lips, my bride, are as sweet as honey. Yes, honey and cream are under your tongue. The scent of your clothing is like that of the mountains and the cedars of Lebanon."*
> (Song of Solomon 4:11 NLT)

Remember, having relationships with us is so important to God that He gave Adam and Eve freedom to make their own choices, at the cost of the horror of the fall, so that He would be able to have real relationships with mankind where we choose to know and love, choose to be known and be loved. And it's still what God wants with us. Rather than a Textbook Wife who imposes harsh regulations on herself to win love, He wants you to believe He is good, and to be trusted, so you can be real and vulnerable and truly yourself with Him.

Open With God

Now I really want to open myself and my life to God and I try to share everything with Him. Sometimes I still catch myself busily working something out in my mind or nursing a wound and I take it to God. I imagine myself face to face with Jesus because it helps me uncover the things that are inside me that really matter so I can speak to Him about them.

What do you think stands in the way of you being your truest self with God? What are you hiding?

If you need reassurance that it's alright to be completely open with God, look at the psalms. The writers communicate from the very depths of their hearts. Whatever the emotion, and however ugly, whether they were joyful, depressed, angry, lonely or afraid, they wrote about it. It is often in the midst of expressing themselves fully and freely, getting things off their chests, that they are brought into greater faith and praise.

David spoke from experience when He advised:

> *"Trust in, lean on, rely on, and have confidence in Him at all times, you people;* ***pour out your hearts*** *before Him."*
> (Psalm 62:8 AMP)

Even Jesus was real with God. He shared from the depths of His being before His crucifixion. He knew what God's will was and He found it immensely hard to go through but He didn't hide how He felt from His Father. It was to God He went, to *"Abba, Father"* (=Daddy) (Mark 14:36 NLT), falling face down on the ground in the place of prayer. *He was in such agony of spirit that his sweat fell to the ground like great drops of blood* (Luke 22:44 NLT).

Three times He pleaded with God to take away this *"cup of suffering"* but each time He emphasised: *"I want your will, not mine"* (Mark 14:36 NLT).

So be real with Him and:

> *Please God, not in a* **dogged religious plod,** *but in a* **living, spirited dance.**
> (1Thessalonians 4:2 MSG)

15

THE HOW TO: Your Relationship Moment By Moment

Once you see that you are offered a love that can totally satisfy, from someone you can trust and be your truest self with, rather than feeling that you *really should* pray/ read your Bible/ go to church/ worship and obey God, you *actually want* to know HOW TO do whatever will enable you to be as intimate with Him as it is possible to be. In the next two chapters, we will consider two ways of having the closest relationship with God that you can.

The first is to begin to live conscious of Jesus' 24/7 presence with you. **Enjoying relationship with Jesus is unlike relating to anybody else because He is always within you.** That means you can turn to Him first always. Talk to Him first, ask His opinion first, seek His approval first, ask for His advice first. The ultimate person to person interaction can literally happen moment by moment of every night and day.

Jesus calls you His *friend* (John 15:15). And friends hang out together. We develop the friendship as we include Jesus in everything we do from the most mundane to the most exciting things. Jesus invites us:

> *Look! Here I stand at the door and knock. If you hear me calling and open the door, I will come in and we will **share a meal as friends**.*
> (Revelation 4:20 NLT)

That's no more lonely lunches, breakfasts, suppers!

107

It can be hard to fill your mind with Jesus all the time when it is so in contrast to the old habit of going about life with Him left out altogether or only called upon at certain times. However, there is always something going on in your mind. As you think, you kind of hold conversations with yourself. So how about redirecting that communication and starting to talk to Jesus instead and listening as He talks back?

Relationship is about two-way conversation and **Jesus wants to talk to you**. That makes a lot of people feel worried that they won't hear Him right. If you are someone who doubts she can hear Jesus, be assured that you actually can! You have been given the *capacity to hear* (Psalm 40:6 AMP). Begin to ask Him questions and allow replies to form that are what you think He would say. You'll soon find that you are chatting away as you become more focused on Him than you are on yourself.

However, be careful with this! You are not Jesus!!

Jesus modelled this way of living Himself. He was in the closest, unbroken communication with God. He tells us so many times that He never did or said anything unless it was His Father's will: *"I do nothing of Myself (of my own accord or on My own authority), but I say [exactly] what My Father has taught Me"* (John 8:28 AMP).

Friends Spending Time Together

Jesus never leaves us. We really can live our lives with HIM doing everything—the mundane, the spiritual, the extraordinary—TOGETHER. How that looks for you is going to be unique for you. God wants to enjoy something totally different with each person He's made but it may interest and encourage you to see a glimpse of how it is for other people:

1960's Evenings With Jesus

Sylvia Mary Allison discovered the joy of spending her time with Jesus. Throughout the 1960's, she spent a lot of lonely evenings on her own and she would often sink into deep depressions. She says that she was 'beyond tears', lying on her bed, staring at the ceiling for hours. She would phone people because she didn't want to be alone and she heard Jesus say: "You are not alone: I am with you. I am your husband: talk to me." She replied: "I don't want to be rude, Lord, but I don't think I could talk to you for the whole evening." However, she decided to try it so she sat in a chair, pretending Jesus was sitting in the chair opposite her, and she started to talk to Him. She says that she discovered many things:

'Both people need to talk and listen... after a time I dried up so I began to ask Him what He thought... new thoughts came into my mind, bits of Scripture'. She also learned: 'that if you love someone, you don't have to talk, or be talked to, all the time. You can just sit in silence and enjoy each other's company'. Her depression when 'alone' lifted.[50]

The Seventeenth Century French Monastery With Jesus

The Seventeenth Century monk, Brother Lawrence, wrote about his lifestyle of focusing on God's presence **within** himself, and how he would talk lovingly to Him and enjoy His company all the time: 'every moment, without rule or restriction, above all at times of temptation, distress, dryness, and revulsion, and even of faithlessness and sin'.

He recommends that we would: 'turn at every moment to Him and ask for His help,... offering what we do to him before we do it and giving thanks for having done it afterwards. In this unbroken communion one is continually preoccupied with praising, worshipping and loving God for his infinite acts of loving-kindness and perfection.

My happiness keeps growing. I sense joys so unbroken and so great that I have difficulty in restraining them'.[51]

Public Places With Jesus

Jesse Duplantis describes his friendship with Jesus:

'The first thing I say when I get up in the morning is "Hey, Jesus." He says, "Hey, Jesse." Passion begins in a personal

relationship with Jesus... I know Him. Sometimes I forget I'm
in a public place and talk to Him out loud. "Jesus, listen, what
do you think about that?"

realness with

"Really, did I just hear you say what I think I heard you say?" *Jesus*
People look at me strange, but prayer is a very simple thing for
me because it's personal'.[52]

honesty

I wanna be like that!

A Working Day With Jesus

In a talk I heard him give, Bill Hybels describes how to spend your whole day
with Jesus from beginning to end. He says that when the alarm clock goes off
first thing, we can either start the day with Jesus or not! We may be used to
saying our first expletive of the day, hitting the alarm, jumping out of bed and
running to the shower but there is another way! He suggests we stop the
alarm and say: "Good Morning God. Here is a day that you've invited me to
do together with you – and my answer is yes! I want to do this day with you."

Because Bill is a very active person and easily able to run through the day at
high speed without being conscious of God's presence with him, he tends to
hit the floor with his knees first, put his hands on the bed and surrender the
day to God's leadership and companionship, aware of the fact that he can't
redo yesterday or live tomorrow yet – it is all about **TODAY with God**.

After a shower, he will eat breakfast and he likes to connect physical eating
with spiritual nourishment by asking God to nourish his soul while the
food nourishes his body.

Next he reads the newspaper. He used to look at it and think how messed
up the world and its leaders are but now he tries to pray through the paper
'bringing God's heart to bear on what's happening in the news'.

At some point he advises that we open the Bible and allow our minds to be
washed with God's words, changing our thoughts and shaping our desires,
listening to what God is saying to us.

On the way to work, rather than listening to troubling things that make him arrive troubled, he listens to worship music so that he arrives with the Spirit of God in his mind. He says that most workplaces are so competitive and Godless, they desperately need the Spirit of Christ and we can bring that.

The Bible says that we should work to God's glory and Bill says that when we do work with Jesus in mind, for His honour, we'll work better than for any individual and we'll be really productive and industrious.

He says that lunchtime provides us with a choice of what we will do. Will we have it alone with God, talking to Him? Or will we have an evangelistic attempt – having lunch with friends and seeing if the Holy Spirit opens some doors in the conversation to talk about God? Or will we have a fellowship lunch with some other Christians? He says that every lunchtime can count!

He encourages us to get into the habit of listening to a conversation with one ear while keeping the other ear open to God. That way God can encourage, rebuke, guide us, even warn us a person is lying. Or when we ask how someone is, and they say that they are fine, He can whisper that they are not really OK. Then we can ask them whether they're sure they're alright and they are given the opportunity to tell us about their struggles.

In the evening, he says that rather than filling our minds with endless TV shows, we could switch the television off half an hour earlier than usual and spend some time reading a book by a man or woman who's learnt some things about God that will help us.

He says: 'When the last thoughts of our day are transcendent thoughts – thoughts about our great God and His kingdom and what He's doing in this world – you know what happens? Your last thought of the day is: "Goodnight God."' Then you think back and you realise: 'We did this whole day together. We spent a day doing this thing called life together'.[53]

Playtime With Jesus

Juan Carlos Ortiz enjoys family life with Jesus:

> 'I believe that one of the greatest inheritances we can give our

children is that we are not activity-oriented Christians. By that I mean that Christ is not something for Tuesdays, Thursdays at 7.30pm and Sundays at 10.00 am, or from 6.00 to 6.30 in the mornings. No, Christ is 24 hours a day. We are in a continual dialogue with that inner Christ. It is continual fellowship because we have become one.

So when my children and I are playing soccer, or while we are doing anything together, we stop in the break and we say, "How nice is this day. We're having fun, aren't we?"

They tell me that they are having great fun. So I say, "Let's tell God, so He can be glad."

Then I say, "Lord, we are having fun, thanks to You."

We don't close our eyes and make it a religious act. In fact, there isn't one instance of anyone closing his eyes to pray anywhere in the Bible (although of course it's all right to do so if we want to). We just talk with God naturally, and we recognise Him in everything. So my children have learned to have a relationship and not a religion'.[54]

Shopping With Jesus

My own experience of clothes shopping with Jesus:

Thank God, I have learned that I can enjoy everything with God and consult with Him over every decision in my life. On one occasion I was shopping for a belt and had found one I really liked but the right size had sold out of the shop. I tried to locate one – going to a couple of other branches where there was a chance of one being in stock. But eventually(!) I paused and thought perhaps this belt wasn't the best thing. So I asked God what I should do and He told me a completely different shop to go to and that I'd find something if I went. It was a most unlikely place to have a nice belt and I wondered if I'd heard right but the words of Jesus to His disciples: "My sheep hear my voice" (John 10:27) came to me and settled my mind so I went to look. And there was a lovely belt – the same style as the one I'd liked in the other chain of shops but far, far nicer and cheaper too! I'd learned that I could have saved a lot of time and trouble if I'd just asked God in the beginning!!!

Hong Kong's Drug Dens And Brothels With Jesus

Jackie Pullinger describes her moment by moment relationship with Jesus:

> 'A delightful American sailor once took me to task about my praying in tongues… he felt it should only be used sparingly for spiritual highs and for special occasions. I explained to him that one reason why God was able to use me was because I kept in touch through using this gift all the time. I prayed in the Spirit as I went around the colony – in buses, on boats, and walking along the streets, very quietly under my breath. **That way it is possible to pray all the time**'.[55]

Jackie offers to take the sailor on a day-long tour of Hong Kong's drug dens and brothels while they pray continuously, aloud but quietly so no one can hear, stopping only to eat and talk to people they meet along the way. These people are converted as she tells them about Jesus, renouncing their old lifestyles. After this, the sailor needed no more convincing about praying in the Holy Spirit.

Jackie finds that she can easily stay in constant communication with Jesus, that moment by moment connection we were talking about, by relying on the Holy Spirit to pray through her. Paul prayed and sang – with his *spirit [by the Holy Spirit that is within me], and also [intelligently] with his mind and understanding* (1Corinthians 4:15 AMP).

Whether or not you felt anything happen, when you asked God to take away your shame and fill you with His Spirit, if you asked sincerely, then by faith, you can thank Him that His Spirit lives within you. And as He lives inside you, you can allow the Spirit to communicate with God through you – in His own sounds and words. A speaker I heard said that he desperately wanted the Holy Spirit to pray through him but he would open his mouth and… nothing! It just didn't happen. He was told to try running through the alphabet and allowing the Spirit to form a word beginning with each letter. As he relaxed and practised, sounds began to form.

Talk to Jesus about praying like this and generally about your desire to live with Him moment by moment. You've seen how a few other people enjoy Jesus' company. Ask him that you would have real companionship the unique way He's designed it for you and Him.

Imagine everyday being a day where you wake up unable to wait for the day to begin – excited about what it will bring!!! That's the life that's on offer to all mankind when we live the way we've been made to – in relationship with God.

16

THE HOW TO: Your Relationship In Private

Taste And See That The Lord Is Good (Psalm 34:8 NLT)

Jesus often withdrew to lonely places and prayed (Luke 5:16 NIV) and He advises us: *"But when you pray, go away by yourself, shut the door behind you, and pray to your Father secretly. Then your Father, who knows all secrets, will reward you"* (Matthew 6:6 NLT). We can live in companionship with Jesus moment by moment but building a relationship is helped by us following His own example, spending specific time on our own, enjoying His presence, and praying, in a more intimate way.

Jesus' disciples walked with Him every day but when it came to prayer, they asked Him to teach them how to do it (Luke 11:1). We can do the same. We can ask Jesus to show us how to spend time with Him in the way that's right for us, that will work for the way we've been made. Ask Him to help you find time and space to spend with Him the way He'd enjoy and you'd enjoy.

The Bible

You saw in the last chapter how people walk with Jesus, and have come to know Him better, in different ways. One way we can all find companionship with Jesus is through reading the Bible. This is not about reading your Bible like some old book that will give you more knowledge but seeing that it is God's own words which are alive and exciting. It's the place where you can expect to fellowship, converse and connect with God. You can open your Bible and say to the Holy Spirit: "I want to fellowship with Jesus through His word."

It's in reading the Bible that your mind will be renewed and your thoughts will line up more and more with God's. As this happens, you'll become clearer when God is speaking to you, that it's actually Him, because you'll be getting to know the kinds of things He'll say.

Rather than it being a boring duty or something you just never get around to, decide to see your Bible in a new way. Start to value and enjoy it. And relax about it. It is a complete joy and privilege to even have a Bible. We come alive as God quickens His word to us and His thoughts and answers are there.

Comfort, direction, instruction, enlightenment. God never fails to deliver what we need and He uses His written Word powerfully. It's so amazing the way that words on paper can be brought to life by the Holy Spirit, speaking deeply into our hearts. If that's not the experience you have of reading your Bible, ask God that it would be.

I value the Bible increasingly in my life. I like to read something first thing in the morning, I may read a bit more during the day when I spend time with God and I wouldn't choose to go to sleep without at least reading a verse – usually I read a Psalm. I choose to have a small Bible in my bag and I've got Bibles spread throughout the rooms of the house.

How do you know which bit to read, how much to read, when to read? Quite simply, ask Jesus! A couple of ideas though: you could choose to read a gospel through – a little bit every day – and see Jesus in action on the earth in His human form. He was there in person so you can talk to Him about what it was really like. Or, you could read Acts or one of Paul's letters to find out about life as we are called to do it – as companions of Jesus in the power of the Holy Spirit. Paul is such an encouragement. He's so excited by Jesus, so certain of God's power, so full of expectancy.

Concordance And Cross Referencing

I know these things sound like they'd only be for theological students but as God speaks to you, they can help you glean as much as possible from what He is saying, making your relationship even more dynamic and exciting.

You can check a verse God highlights to you against other translations of the Bible. Or you may have a Bible with footnotes which tells you what other parts of the Bible that verse relates to so you can look them up. If there's a single word God is emphasising, you can look it up in a Concordance to see where it appears in the Bible.

Journal

Keeping a record of the things God says to you, of verses that stand out to you, becomes a real help as you look back through it. I use a different coloured pen when I feel God is saying something so that I can easily flick through and see what He's said.

Sometimes praying with a pen in your hand helps your thinking become clearer. Often our thoughts are only part formed and fragmented but noting them down helps them become more complete. In the past I didn't cope very well when I looked at my circumstances and would often just end up crying. But God helped me to get into the habit of listing all the issues and then running through them with Him – asking Him: "What do you say about this?" "How should I pray about it?"

Thank God, I don't get unhappy like that anymore, but at times, especially if I feel bogged down with a lot of things to sort out, I make a list of all the pressing issues I need to know God's mind on and I ask Him those same questions and note down His answers.

Immersed In God's Presence

A few years ago, God gave me a very specific way to spend time with Him. I had been ill and had been wanting to find a way of relaxing. That desire was in me and when I flicked through Joyce Huggett's book, *Listening to God*, in a bookshop, I knew that this was God's answer. She presents a method of relaxing in God's presence which I have adapted:

Find a comfortable place either in a chair or in/ on your bed. Before you begin, ask God to protect the time you will spend together. You could put on worship music if that helps to focus you but if you do that, aim for a period of complete silence as well.

1. Relax
Tell your muscles to release their tension and be still. Let the peace of God creep down over your head, your arms and hands, through your body and down into your legs and feet. Say into yourself several times: "My arms and legs are heavy." Imagine they are warm and say into yourself several times: "My arms and legs are warm." Then let your breathing deepen. Inhale through your nose into your stomach saying into yourself: "My breathing is deep and regular" and imagine a balloon is filling in your stomach. Then exhale through your mouth imagining the balloon going down and saying: "My breathing is deep and regular." Repeat 10 times. Then say into yourself several times: "My neck and shoulders are heavy" and be conscious of your head and face relaxing. You should feel your body is too heavy to lift.

2. Presence
Become aware of Jesus' presence – it may be you see His arms around you.

3. Surrender
Give all your worries and cares to Jesus. Knowing He offers you His love, reciprocate. Hand over all that you are, possess, do, feel. "Take me and all I have. I surrender myself and all I possess absolutely, entirely, unconditionally and forever to your control. Please enjoy me now. I open my heart to you, please say what you want to and refresh me with your Holy Spirit."

4. Repentance
Ask God to show you anything that isn't right and say you're sorry. It may be that you reflect on the cross and all Jesus has purchased for you as you confess any sin to Him.

5. Forgiveness
Thank Him for Salvation – that you are forgiven and washed clean.

6. Stillness

Now in deep relaxation and stillness, be open to Jesus and experience real intimacy with Him:

> 'You turn yourself entirely to his presence. You steadily look at him. His presence becomes more real to you. He holds your inward sight. Your glance simply and lovingly rests on him. Your prayer is nothing but a loving awareness of him: I look because I love; I look in order to love, and my love is fed and influenced by looking'.[56]

> *Silence is praise to you…*
> *You hear the prayer in it.*
> (Psalm 65:1–2 MSG)

It will probably have taken about 15 minutes to quieten yourself away from the busyness of life and enter into rest. But it may be that you don't get past relaxing and fall asleep and that's fine! Or you may get caught up enjoying Jesus' presence with you for an extended period and then feel ready to get up and go on with your day.

7. Receiving

Having been in a close encounter with Jesus, present any particular needs you have. If any parts of your body need to be healed or strengthened see the light of the Holy Spirit there and see your body well. Request you would be empowered to do all that's required of you.

8. Praise and Thanksgiving

Worship may well up in your heart before this point but praise and thank God for anything that comes particularly to mind.

9. Intercession

Wait on the Holy Spirit to show you who, or what, to pray for and ask whether you can do anything practical to help.

At whatever point you feel your time is finished, there will be a satisfaction in your heart and a release to go and get on with life. Get up and get on with your day with of Jesus.

I decided that it was right for me to spend an hour every day following this method of spending time with God and that's what I did. I remember giving it a start going home on the tube. I shut my eyes and imagined God's presence with me. I could see the Olympic flame. I could have dismissed that outright. It was the time of the Olympics so I could certainly have assumed that was 'just me', nothing to do with God. But I pondered it – this strong flame that never goes out and I sensed my need to receive God's love and have it burning inside me like that.

The next day, I worked through the whole method lying in bed. Relaxing, I could imagine Jesus' hands holding mine, aware of Him with me. Surrendering, I wanted to draw a line under all I had been in the past and give everything to God. I felt led to repent of some of the stress and negativity I'd fallen into on the previous day. And then receiving God's forgiveness, it was as if He was lighting three Olympic flames in me – of faith, hope and love – that wouldn't go out. He was filling me with the warmth of His love.

I found I loved spending time with God like this. Bit by bit He led me through great healing and repentance. He guided me to verses in the Bible. And I met someone in Jesus who really loved me, who made me feel secure and wanted. I could see more and more who He was, His character. He was fun, kind, unconquerable, exciting, sensitive, attentive, devoted, unpredictably creative. He was more than a hero. When I was with Him in these prayer times, I was confident, there was absolutely nothing to fear. He made me feel so safe and I knew that together, we were unstoppable. He gave me strength and hope and more happiness than I had ever known. He uncovered things in my heart about who I was and gently enabled me to become the woman He had made me to be.

A Place Of Worship

That method of spending an hour a day with God was specific direction for me. It led me to a place of worship before God which is something we crave (even if we don't know it!) We are made to worship God – to have intense love and admiration, a profound devotion to Him. It is so much a part of our makeup that when we don't worship God, we still find ourselves worshipping something. Man has worshipped many things through history – wooden idols, physical desires, money and possessions, family, friends, lovers, political leaders, success, talents, hobbies, education etc. Any worship that is not directed towards God is dictated and controlled by the devil. So when we don't worship God, we worship the devil.

What do you worship? To see, you need to ask yourself where your priorities lie – what means the most to you, what you give your time and heart to, what you revere and serve, what you focus on.

Kiss The Son (Psalm 2:12 NIV)

Kiss: a touch or pressure given with the lips, in token of affection, greeting, or reverence.
Shorter Oxford English Dictionary

WORSHIP most commonly appears as 'proskuneo' in the New Testament = Greek for 'to kiss towards'.

> *Worship God in adoring embrace.*
> (Psalm 2 MSG)

For many people, true intimacy with God comes in times of quietness before Him, immersed in Him – experiencing an inner communication without words. It is through these times that God convinces people of His love for them, reveals His deep knowledge of them and leaves them responding with love for Him. Here is a glimpse of different experiences:

Joyce Huggett describes her times of intimacy with God and she says: 'I never know in advance how God is going to meet with me. The Divine Lover sometimes comes as the Father, the one who is saving the best robe for the worst child, the Father who gave his own Son, such is the generosity of his loving. Sometimes my Lord comes as the loving, searching Shepherd, sometimes as life. Sometimes as energy... Sometimes he comes to me as the Bridegroom to his Bride and in that knowing there is such awesome love'.

Entering her prayer room one day when she was feeling especially lonely, she focused on God's presence and says that she saw herself as a 'fragile, helpless, vulnerable' new-born baby cradled in God's arms: 'his finger was stroking my cheek, his eyes were twinkling down at me'. She wasn't alone and it made her feel loved.

She says that she could have read and meditated on verses in the Bible that would have described this, like: *Underneath are the everlasting arms* (Deuteronomy 33:27 NIV), or *I have loved you with an everlasting love* (Jeremiah 31:3 NIV). But it was seeing the arms and experiencing the love that was so wonderful and powerful for her.

— Joyce Huggett[57]

★　★　★

'Once I was sitting very relaxed when I sensed God say: "Martha." I knew just what He meant. I hadn't chosen the better part as Mary had. Then I saw I was tapping at an old farm house door. I walked in, to the back scullery where the servants would work. The walls were stone, glistening and running with cold dampness. I said, "Why am I standing here?" "That's you." God said, "You let the cares and anxieties stay with you until they seep into your innermost being."

I was then led out of the scullery. There was a beautiful room with a large table spread out with every kind of food. God said, "This is always there for you to come to, but you choose the back kitchen." We moved on to a sitting room where there was a tremendous sense of peace. I drew back. The voice said gently, "I'm always here, waiting for you."

I thought that was the end. But there was another room, even larger, with a bright crystal chandelier reflecting in the polished wooden floor. As a girl I had never been allowed to go to dances; that was something we Christians didn't do. Now I was dancing in the ballroom with Jesus and it was amazing. I'm 78 and enjoying life more than ever'.

— Rebecca[58]

★　★　★

I was in my mother's womb, God was stroking my head and I was just feeling loved. This was the first time I really received Father God's love.

– Anne Hibbert[59]

★ ★ ★

When I first started to spend time with Jesus in the way described in this chapter, I found myself in different scenarios with Him. One day it was as if we went up mountains and Jesus told me He'd made all of it. We both had some clay and He made a perfect replica of a flower and I made something too. The word strongly imprinted on my mind was 'ENJOY!' I was being given liberty to enjoy the world.

I had other amazing experiences of being on safari with Jesus and stroking lions, being on the beach and swimming and diving in the sea in a way I wouldn't naturally be able, or dare, to do.

It was as if God was laying the world at my feet, inviting me into His home and garden, a bit like in this Psalm:

> *We all arrive at your doorstep sooner*
> *or later,...*
> *Blessed the guest*
> *at home in your place!*
> *All your salvation wonders*
> *are on display in your trophy room.*
> *Earth-Tamer, Ocean-Pourer,*
> *Mountain-Maker, Hill-Dresser...*
> (Psalm 65 MSG)

– Anna Symonds

★ ★ ★

In an article about her prayer times, Jackie Pullinger says:

'I always start sunbathing. That's what prayer is like! I turn my face to God like you turn your face to the sun... I have a list of things to talk to Him about but I never get to the list, because He spends nearly all the time saying how beautiful I am. He's extravagant about me, and I get embarrassed. I say: "Thank you very much! Could we talk about work?"

And He usually says: "No, I want to tell you how much I love you!"...
most of my prayer time is sunbathing in God's approval'.

★ ★ ★

Derek Prince talks of how he and his wife would praise God and the 'loud,
jubilant, excited praise brings us into the presence of God... then our
response to Him changes. It is no longer the utterance of thanksgiving and
praise but an attitude of reverence and worship in the presence of Almighty
God, in which we are open to hear His voice. With our spirits quiet before
God, He speaks to us. We have had much direction, warning, and
encouragement from Him in these times.'

Prince describes these quiet times as WORSHIP – spiritual union – your
spirit united with God's Spirit – the climax of praise and thanksgiving. And
out of this comes fruitfulness, just as human physical union leads to
reproduction.[60]

★ ★ ★

John Eldredge says: 'We worship sex because we don't know how to
worship God... But our hearts live for 'an experience of worship that fills
our beings with a joy that is so deeply in awe of the other that we are barely
aware of ourselves.' Many people have a hard time conceiving of this kind
of intimacy with God. For their entire lives they have related to Him in a
distant, though reverent way'.[61]

★ ★ ★

'A handful of years ago, I found myself in what you might call a Holy Spirit
ministry service. As we worshipped and embraced the luxury of lingering
in His presence, I felt as though I was at the door of the Throne Room of
God. It wasn't a 'full-on, Panasonic colour type' vision, but it was a very
strong impression that changed not only me, but many others who I have
shared it with. It was as though I was on the threshold of the Throne
Room, my toes on the edge and I was peeking in. I then sensed the Holy
Spirit come alongside (as He does) and nudge me. He very gently said,
"You can go in, you know. You can go in. Sit at his feet. Sit on His knee if

you want... and He will tell you everything you need to know." That vision, impression, encounter – call it what you wish – has fed my spirit many times. It has sustained me in my journey and encouraged me many times to draw aside and find the fuel, gold or food needful'.

– Bobbie Houston[62]

The message to you is the same. God is inviting you into His presence, to a place of intimacy and worship.

17

THE HOW TO: More On Your Relationship In Private

Your relationship with God belongs to you and Him. This book isn't meant to be about you reading and absorbing mine or anyone else's experiences and seeking to make them your own. Rather it's meant to be an encouragement to find your own living and true relationship with Jesus and to go about that in whatever way is right for you. It's about writing yourself into your own love story, your own life story, with God.

If you decide that you want to try resting in His presence, even if just for 5 minutes as you relax and let the Holy Spirit minister to you, you have the guide in the previous chapter. There is some further advice below relating to situations that may be brought up through your prayer time:

The Uncertainties

Often people say things like: "God didn't speak to me." "I couldn't feel His presence." "I just heard the central heating gurgling." "I couldn't focus on Jesus." "I had a completely inappropriate tune in my head." "My mind was wandering all over the place." "All I could see was the pile of work I need to do." "I thought God was telling me things but how do I know it was God and not just me inventing it?"

If you feel anything like any of that, here are a few pointers to help you:

- You need to focus on the fact that God is within you, that He wants to talk to you and for you to hear Him. Ask Him to help you discern

His voice. Tell Him what scares you about it and the doubts you have.

- Remember, anything God says to you will never, ever contradict the Bible.

- There is a freshness to it when God speaks. It goes to the heart of you, better than anything you could make up yourself, often bringing a supernatural invasion of peace.

- Keep a note of what God says and any Bible verses He guides you to. I often find that if something is important, God makes sure that I hear it again and again. Perhaps it will come up in my Bible reading, in a sermon at church, in something somebody says to me or in some other way.

- You are giving Him your time and self with your love so relax and welcome what He wants to give. You can end up dismissing the whispers of God by saying that they're 'just you' and overlooking what God is wanting to say to you. Hold a picture you can see, hold a sound or lyric you can hear – even a seemingly completely inappropriate one – and ask God what the thought is behind the thought. For example, don't dismiss the pile of work you can see – perhaps God is wanting to talk to you about that work or just get you to leave it for a few minutes while He takes you deeper into Himself. Turn the focus back to Him continuously. The devil wants to stop you having companionship with God so deny him his pleasure and press on confidently regardless of your doubts and fears.

- Sometimes you may feel God's presence in a tangible way. It is so personal how you feel it – maybe in warmth, your eyelids flickering, a deep peace, a heaviness, a tingling. Other times you may feel nothing at all which doesn't mean God isn't there. God is within you 24/7. Full stop. Feeling or not feeling it physically doesn't change His presence being with you.

- As you spend time in Jesus' presence, you may find your heart overflowing with love and worship. Or you may find yourself praying in the Spirit – with words you don't know or even groans or sighs or heavy breathing. Paul describes this:

And the Holy Spirit helps us in our distress. For we don't even know what we should pray for, nor how we should pray. **But the Holy Spirit prays for us with groanings that cannot be expressed in words.** *And the Father who knows all hearts knows what the Spirit is saying, for the Spirit pleads for us believers in harmony with God's own will.*

(Romans 8:26-28 NLT)

Bringing Healing And Release From Sin

As you rest in Jesus' presence, you may find that He is leading you into greater freedom and peace by touching deep places within you. He may draw your awareness to problems or griefs that you have (maybe even to things you weren't aware of) to gently bring healing and release. He knows the best way to lead you to freedom so welcome the healing on offer.

Here's how to take action if He is prompting you to ask for forgiveness and to renounce something in your life that isn't right:

1.   Tell God how you feel – the truth of the pain or the problem.

2.   Take some time to ask God what is at the root of a problem. A word may form in your mind – 'resentment', 'self-pity', 'hatred' – that is the Holy Spirit revealing the identity of your enemy. If we fail to exercise self-control and keep giving in to something like fear, we can open the way for a spirit to repeatedly attack us, influencing us and opening the way for other negative spirits to follow.

3.   Call the issues what they are and confess them as sin. Renounce any enemy by name: "I repent of walking in (eg. fear). **In the name of Jesus, I bind** you (eg. spirit of fear). I command you to leave me and I proclaim my release."

4.   Walk in freedom. Ask the Holy Spirit to empower you to walk in the opposite way. If you have renounced fear, say: "Holy Spirit, **in the name of Jesus, I loose** your peace within me. Please empower me to walk in it."

5. Ask God for a verse that speaks of the truth that you are walking in and claim it.

(eg. *"I do not have a spirit of fear..."* (2Timothy 1:7).)

As you begin to open up an issue, God may show you that it goes deeper than you thought. Allow Him to lead you through the process of healing and be aware that this can take time. We have a responsibility to discover the awesome power of God to break patterns of behaviour, even those that have suffocated our family for many years, and claim a new identity and way for the future generations.

Bringing Healing And Release From Wounds

Soon after I started spending time with Jesus in this way it was as if He was taking knives from all over my body and kissing each wound of all the pain that people had inflicted on me. He comforted me and also offered protection against anymore knives that would be thrown – His pierced body would take the pain for me.

This moved me to be able to open my heart to God about all the rejection I had experienced and importantly to forgive people. Many of us find that deep down there are offences we have never properly forgiven. Some of the most difficult things we will have faced will have been problems with other people. God loves them and us too much to allow resentments to remain. He requires us to forgive. Unforgiveness is a barrier to us receiving God's blessing and best for our lives.

I think there are four important stages in forgiving people that can allow you to receive full healing and freedom from the hurt. These four stages completely freed me from the pain I had regarding one person who still affected me emotionally nearly two years after I'd last seen them. I thought I'd forgiven them but I'd only done step 2 and it wasn't enough for me to have really let the pain go.

1. Open your heart to God about what has been done to you by the person. Don't hold back – in the Psalms, David brought His innermost, and most negative, feelings about other people to God.

You can repent too for any bitterness you've harboured against the person.

2. Think of the person you need to forgive, close your eyes and picture them with Jesus. Consider that He died for them just like He did for you. When you see them in that way, there is no option left but to say: "I forgive   X   in the name of Jesus. And I give thanks that   X   is forgiven."

3. Pray for the person to be blessed. Say: "I bless   X   in Jesus' name." Ask God to love them through you from now on – it may or may not be someone you will ever have to see again.

4. Choose to forget their offence against you and start to speak well of them.

speak well of everyone!

Bringing Healing And Release From The Painful Past

Jesus may touch places of past wounding within you that He wants to revisit so He can bring freedom and healing to fear and pain. He invites you to hand over your ashes of the past and trade them in for His comfort and a transformed future.

God has known, and kept a record of, all your tears:

> *You keep track of all my sorrows.*
> *You have collected all my tears in a bottle.*
> **You have recorded each one** *in your book.*
> (Psalm 56:8 NLT)

And He will transform the tears:

> *Those who plant in tears*
> *will harvest with shouts of joy.*
> *They weep as they go to plant their seed,*
> *but they sing as they return with the harvest.*
> (Psalm 126:5–6 NLT)

God's will for you is "beauty for ashes" – the restoration of all that the devil has tried to steal:

> *The rains He sends are an expression of His grace. Once more the autumn rains will come, as well as the rains of spring. The threshing floors will again be piled high with grain, and the presses will overflow with wine and olive oil. The Lord says,* **"I will give you back what you lost to the stripping locusts, the cutting locusts, the swarming locusts, and the hopping locusts."**
> (Joel 2:23-25 NLT)

> *He also turns deserts into pools of water,*
> *the dry land into flowing springs.*
> *He brings the hungry to settle there*
> *and build their cities.*
> *They sow their fields, plant their vineyards,*
> *and* **harvest their bumper crops.**
> *How He blesses them!*
> (Psalm 107:35-38 NLT)

We can't live in the past and receive the bright future God has planned at the same time. Jesus wants us to let go of what lies behind and start enjoying the new life He has for us. Our memories can put us on the road to despair but they don't have to – we can live in peace with the past. You can let all your history become His Story as you watch God transform your life whatever has gone before.

God who has a perfect memory says He chooses to suspend it: *"I... am the one who blots out your sins for my own sake and will never think of them again"* (Isaiah 43:25 NLT). That gives us freedom to actually forget the past too. Paul says that's how he lives: *"I am focusing all my energies on this one thing:* **Forgetting the past** *and looking forward to what lies ahead, I strain to reach the end of the race and receive the prize..."* (Philippians 3:13 NLT).

Giving up the ashes, crying on Jesus, telling Him everything, receiving His forgiveness and forgiving other people all helps us to live free from the past but in my experience, parts of the past remained terribly painful, and there was no true release from them, until I had:

I. Brought Jesus into the painful memory.

In Chapter 6, I told you the story about the woman who realised Jesus had been singing to her while she was locked in the cupboard as a child. That realisation brought her great healing.

When God has allowed really painful memories to come to my mind, things that seemed so far from any light or goodness I couldn't conceive of God's presence in them, I have asked Jesus to come into that memory and what He has then revealed to me has always completely changed the way I have felt about those horrible times.

Agnes Sanford tells the story of a Priest who remembers himself as an unhappy, lonely child of 8. As he invites Jesus to come into that memory, he sees Jesus come up to him and ask if he is alright. He tells Jesus that he is alone and sad. Jesus gets His mother, Mary, who comforts the boy and then asks him if he's happy now. The boy says he is but still lonely for someone to play with.

Mary goes to get Jesus who is also now a little boy of 7 or 8, dressed 'in a rather sissy costume of white robe and sash'. Jesus asks the boy what he enjoys doing and he says he likes to 'skip stones in the brook'.

'So they went down to the brook and skipped stones and played in the water, getting their shoes and all their clothes rather wet. They took off their shoes, and thought it would be fun to exchange them, and then went on to exchange clothes as well, Jesus putting on the little American boy's sailor suit, and he the Lord's white robe. Thus it came to pass that in the vision Jesus stood on the earth in the shoes of a man, and the little boy was clothed in the white robes of righteousness'.[63]

The Priest was healed, through that vision, of a **lifetime of loneliness and depression.**

There was one period of a couple of years (in the time since I had got to know God) that I felt particularly unhappy to think of. God prompted me to make a list of the major things that had happened throughout that time and then against them the things God had revealed about Himself, me and my life; my greater understanding of His truth and deeper love for Him.

That transformed how I felt. The unhappiness of that time faded and I look back on it now with so much genuine amazement and gratefulness.

2. Praised God for it all.

Lord, you are Sovereign, nothing that has happened has been without your permission. You had and have a perfect plan for me and my life and I thank you. Thank you that I was in your mind before I was formed. You thought me up and allowed my conception and growth in the womb and my birth. How wonderful that the greatest designer ever made me. I'm not a Rembrandt or a Picasso worth millions. I'm God made and I'm priceless.

You knew the ways in which the enemy would try to spoil your plans but nothing will stop the good work you have started. Thank you that I was born the way I was into the family I have, looking the way I do and with the gifts, talents, personality and weaknesses that made me. Thank you for my early childhood – all the things I don't remember and those I've been told about. Thank you that you were always there loving me, desiring to bless me and uphold me.

I made a list and praised for all the good things I could remember:

Thank you for all the joys, Lord, all the wonderful things I have loved...

And I made a list and thanked Him for all the things that hadn't been so good!

I also want to thank you for the rest – for the things I have struggled with... and pray you would comfort me.

Thank you Lord that I am who I am and I am where I am how I am. Thank you that your plans go on for me – perfect plans and you will comfort, heal and move me on. You will fulfil promises you have made. Thank you there is always light whatever the seeming darkness. May I live in praise for all your workings in my life from now on.

A prayer of praise like that brings freedom so that you can remember the good and know the rest is forgiven and forgotten. Then you can think of hopes and dreams, not the fears, frustrations, unfulfillment and failure, but all that's still excitingly possible.

If You Take One Thing...

If I could get you to take just one thing from this part of the book, it is that:

<u>**YOU** really are able to have an *amazing* relationship with God.</u>

I don't say that lightly. I have known what it's like to be terrified of being asked to pray out loud in front of other people. I've sat praying to be left out when people have been invited to share things that God has said to them. It can seem as if there are some people who are marked out to be spiritual high flyers – the people at the top of the God class. Certain people who get it. The ones God speaks to. The ones who can hear Him. The ones who do worship the right way. Who pray the right way. Who people look up to as being better at having a relationship with Jesus than everybody else.

But that is rubbish.

The truth about having a relationship with Jesus is that:

* It's for *EVERYBODY*. It is for you, whoever you are, wherever you were born, whatever you have/ haven't done in your life.

* It's easy for *ANYBODY*. You have been *made* to hear Jesus speak and to enjoy His company all day, every day – right now. Not in a few years time when you've had some intense theological training. The more time you spend with Him, listening, the more you'll recognise His voice.

* It's better than anything for *EVERYBODY*. If you make intimacy with Jesus your priority, you will not be disappointed. If you stop searching for fulfilment anywhere but Jesus, you will begin to find a satisfaction you never knew was possible to have.

* *EACH PERSON* matters desperately in it. God cannot have what He would have with you with *anybody else* who has ever lived or will ever live.

So, don't miss out thinking that it's for everybody else to have an amazing relationship with God except you!

The King is wild for YOU.
(Psalm 45:11 MSG)

whole,   free,   alive,   believing,   trusting,

adoring,   rejoicing,   entrusted,   anointed,

empowered,   equipped,   gifted,   capable,

sent,   tenacious,   courageous,   confident,

peaceful,   calm,   assured,   excited,

anticipating,   joyful,   enthused,   passionate,

decisive,   strong,   intelligent,

wise,   inspired,   creative,   impacting,

loyal,   kind,   generous,   fun,   warm,

inspirational,   authentic,   genuine,   flourishing,

REALLY LIVING

18

Free To Become

In your generous love I am **REALLY LIVING** *at last.*

(Psalm 63:3 MSG)

Living in relationship with Jesus is our calling and purpose and out of that intimacy comes the ultimate way of life: really living as we take part, *with* Him, in the things He wants to do on the Earth! God is calling us:

> *Into companionship* **and PARTICIPATION** *with His Son, Jesus.*
>
> (1 Corinthians 1:9 AMP)

You are personally invited to partner with Jesus, to take your place by His side as you work TOGETHER! He says: "Join me!" He sees you in the crowd of billions who live on this Earth and He picks you out for a unique and special role. You qualify just because you're you, just the way you are – there's no need for a CV or interview!

So in this part of the book, you're going to be finding out from Jesus what He wants you to be a part of with Him, the things that you alone have been created for – the good life that has long been planned for you to live. Remember, you have been:

> *Recreated in Christ Jesus that you may do those* **good works which I predestined** *(planned beforehand) for you (taking* **paths which I prepared** *ahead of time) that you should walk in them (living the* **good life which I prearranged** *and made ready for you to live).*
>
> (Ephesians 2:10 AMP)

The Voices That Influence Us

"So, what do you want to be when you grow up?"

When you were asked that question, did you know the answer? Did you grow up with a dream? Did you say that you didn't know what you wanted to be? Or did you make something up to keep people quiet?

The questions don't end when we leave school. "What's next?" seems to shape so much of our lives. No sooner are we through exams than we're picking another course, going to interviews, changing job contracts, moving house, starting a different relationship. And then watching our children and grandchildren navigate the pattern.

Most of us don't grow up realising that God actually has a plan for our lives and even if we do have some idea of that, we may not know how to hear His voice above all the other voices that influence the way we see our lives and help us work out the steps to take.

I grew up very uncertain about what I was going to become. I remember all kinds of things that were said to me, many by well meaning people. I think that many of the voices in my life were motivated by a genuine desire to see me fulfill my potential but they spoke with no awareness of God's purposes for me. And although I could laugh off all the input I didn't agree with, I'm sure it went into my mind and influenced the way I saw my future – what seemed to make a life worthwhile.

God says: *"I will guide you along the best pathway for your life"* (Psalm 32:8 NLT). But in order to receive that direction, we need to change our way of thinking:

> Let God transform you… by changing the way you think. **Then you will know what God wants you to do**, and you will know how good and pleasing and perfect His will really is.
> (Romans 12:2 NLT)

Our way of thinking can be changed as we recognise what has been directing us up until now.

TESTS AND GUIDE BOOKS

In modern society there is a lot of emphasis on doing personality tests and career tests, reading books and following computer programmes that we look to for answers. We want them to tell us if we're gifted at this, this and this and have a certain kind of personality, what we should do with our lives. Sometimes God may use one of those tests in someone's life but we must be aware that unless we're specifically directed there by the Holy Spirit, they're not the place to go to for answers

Think for a minute about any career or personality tests you've done. Have you read dating manuals, relationship guidebooks, self-help books, life coaching manuals, philosophical or religious guides to doing life? We're bombarded by newspapers, magazines, TV etc. with all sorts of advice that doesn't originate with God and it can clutter our minds.

CULTURE, EDUCATION, FAMILY BACKGROUND

The culture, education and family background we live in has shaped the way we see things too, giving us so many ideas about 'success' and 'failure'. We become boxed ourselves and box others, without even realising it, with both positive and negative suggestions, like:

- "It's hard for women to know how to approach getting a career because in the back of their minds they wonder how it will be affected by them giving it up later to have children."
- "All Chinese people are good at Maths."
- "It may be boring but it will be worth it because you'll make a lot of money."
- "People like us don't go to those sort of places."
- "None of our family are artistic. We don't go into creative fields."
- "That's no job for a woman."
- "You've got plenty of time in the future to follow your dreams. Now, you need to knuckle down and get on with what you're doing."
- "This is a rowing school. Everyone who comes here is expected to enjoy rowing."
- "You'll never get a good job if you don't go to university."

But none of these things actually has anything to do with what God says.

OCCULT DIRECTION

Have you been a fan of horoscopes? Have you been involved in attempts to contact the dead, been hypnotised, been to clairvoyants, had your palm, handwriting, tea leaves or tarot read? This is the occult and it amounts to seeking supernatural knowledge from the devil which God tells us not to do:

> Let no one be found among you who... **practices divination** [discovering future events or unknown things by supernatural powers]... **interprets omens** [a thing or occurrence regarded as a sign of future happiness or disaster],... **casts spells**, or who is a **medium** or **spiritisit** or who **consults the dead**. Anyone who does these things is detestable to the Lord.
>
> (Deuteronomy 18:109-12 NIV)

Your Growing Up Story

As you seek God for the destiny He has for you, you may want to begin by considering why you've become the woman you have. There are some questions below to help you run back through your life and see what's influenced you. Where have you given away your identity? Where has fear of what people think, illness, grief, circumstances, lack of finances or education stolen who you wanted to be? Did you ever know who you wanted to be anyway or have the things you've gravitated towards been because you didn't know God's heart for you?

However low you feel you've come, however far from who you truly are, you can and will become the woman you were made to be! Jesus wants that for you and He will heal the hurts and transform your situation.

First of all, think back to when you were a child. Do you have memories of being appreciated by parents, family, friends, teachers, of particular compliments or encouragement that you took to heart and moulded what you saw your strengths to be?

Where did you fail? Where were you told you were no good or received bad marks that shaped how you perceived your weaknesses?

Sports; my parents always used to mock me saying, "Oh no. I broke a nail." Common sense; I get called a dizzy blonde & I don't know how to be domestic.

Who do you think you felt that you were by the end of school? When you decided what to do next, did it come from your heart or were your deepest desires becoming lost? Or did external circumstances takes over?

By the end of school I was anorexic. I didn't really know who I was. I looked for myself anywhere. I went to college so I could take drama, something I'd wanted to do from 14, but lost

What about the rest of your life? What has significantly shaped the person *the* you've become – parents, circumstances in your life, your partner, children, *passion* friends, tutors, specialist, boss, colleagues, work environment, church, family identity, nationality, the media…?

Home & parents- not happy, now divorced.
Friends - becoming like them at school.
Boys- always have to have a boyfriend.
The media- looking for myself in those I admire.

Free!

My cousin told me about a friend of his whose wife had been studying the effect on a person's adult life of the command/expectation that dominated their childhood. The friend's wife saw herself as: "Be perfect" – always as a child feeling that she had to perform to be loved and as an adult paranoid about making everything just right.

I asked God about this. As His daughters, what "Be…" should show in our lives, and He seemed to say: "Be free" which corresponds to the Bible where it says that: *It is for freedom that Christ has set us free!* (Galatians 5:1 NIV).

That's really important for us to take on board. Jesus has won freedom for us. We're no longer captives to sin or the devil, to the past, to anything.

Whatever you have done in your life, however far you have strayed from God's ways and from the destiny that He has for you, you are completely free now to become the woman God desires you to be.

If you want to live the life that God has planned for you, just tell Him that you're sorry for going to other sources for direction. Tell Him you want Him to clear away any influences getting in the way of you discerning His voice and will. Release the pressures and fears that have affected you and ask for God's mindset, that He'd rid you of your own preconceptions and swap them for His vision. Ask Him if there are any books etc. that have guided you that He wants you to throw out, even destroy.

> *I'm happy from the inside out,*
> *And from the outside in,…*
>
> *Now you've got my feet on the life path,*
> *All radiant from the shining of your face.*
> *Ever since you took my hand,*
> **I'm on the right way.**
>
> (Psalm 16:9-11 MSG)

planned, designed, conceived, individual, priceless, valued, adored, desired,

confident, peaceful, calm, assured, courageous, gifted, fun,

pursued, esteemed, beloved, purchased, unconditionally loved, accepted, forgiven, adopted, restored, alive,

empowered, equipped, sent, entrusted, purposed, excited, anticipating, joyful, enthused, loyal,

delighted in, special, believing, trusting, adoring, rejoicing, lovely, beautiful, radiant, irresistible, real,

creative, generous, capable, relaxed, smiling, eager, loyal, warm, genuine, flourishing,

GOD

REWROTE THE TEXT

OF MY LIFE

WHEN I OPENED

THE BOOK OF MY

HEART TO HIS EYES

(Psalm 18:24 MSG)

passionate, decisive, strong, wise, inspired, kind,

whole, free, worthy, precious, watched over, protected, prospered,

19

Free To Dream

Once you are aware of the things that have influenced the path you've taken, you can begin to ask the right questions of the right person!

God created you on purpose for a purpose. He planned you to live now and has made you a certain way, with specific talents, to do great things with Him! And the seeds of those great things are already planted as dreams in your heart.

When we hear that, we can feel afraid because we feel empty inside, as if there's nothing there – no dreams, no future, no destiny. And that's exactly the way the devil wants it – to steal our dreams and vision and box us in with fears and uncertainties. But don't feel cast down. God does have a good plan for YOUR life. YOU do have a significant part to play in His purposes.

Afraid To Desire

Some of the feeling empty of dreams can actually be because we fear our desires. Many of us think that what we want couldn't possibly be what God wants. We think: "It's all me, it's not God. The things I want are bad. My ideas are bad."

But that's not the case. Our desires matter to God. Often when I have asked God what He wants me to do, He has replied by asking me what I want to do. My stomach used to turn at the thought of following my heart. It filled me with guilt. I equated doing God's will with painful sacrifice so I tried to ignore or suppress things I thought I wanted.

God told me that was actually self-abuse. I was quenching His Spirit within me – I wasn't allowing Him to guide me. As we lay down our old agenda and decide we want to live the life God has planned, we have to take our desires very seriously, however random or irrelevant they seem.

Rather than seeing ourselves separately from God, we need to focus on the fact that His Spirit lives within us. Many of our longings are because we are made in the image of God. They get distorted through being fallen but as you desire to do God's will, you will think and dream because of God, not apart from Him. Your passions will be redirected – driven by new and different values.

SOME DESIRES THAT ORIGINATE WITH GOD BUT GET DISTORTED THROUGH BEING FALLEN		
Desire to:	**Originates with God:**	**Distorted through fall can lead to:**
Be loved, adored, pursued, wanted, enjoyed, delighted in – not for anything we can do, or give, or be – but just for who we are.	Isn't that exactly what God offers?	Obsessive pursuit of human love to provide fulfillment.
Be in love – giving our whole heart and passion.	Isn't that exactly the way we can be with God?	Having idols – worshipping a man, ✗ career, children, money etc.
Be fascinated, awestruck, filled with wonder, discovering new and exciting things, having adventure.	Isn't that exactly what a life focused on God is all about?	Becoming a thrill seeker. Using travel, sport, money, entertainment, education to fill the hole inside.
Be truly beautiful, to have glory instead of shame.	Isn't that exactly what we are made to be?	An unhealthy desperation over physical appearance,

		yearning to be a size 00 etc.
Be great, noble, successful, ruling, powerful, impacting the lives of others.	Isn't that exactly who we are made to be as Jesus reveals Himself to the world through us?	It may lead a fallen woman to become arrogant and ruthless.
Live forever.	Isn't that exactly how God made us – to desire eternal life?	Fear of death drives the anti-ageing industry.

What are the desires in your heart?

What are the desires in your heart? There are some questions below to help you think it through. Don't worry if you don't have an answer or you think what you want could never be achieved. Just allow yourself the freedom to dream:

What do I really love? It may be places, hobbies, people, anything. Somewhere in that is likely to be a clue to what God has designed you to do.

Seeing people on fire for God; meeting people I can really respect and look up to. Clothes & fashion. Travel.

What do I hate? Somewhere in that is likely to be a clue to what God's placed on your heart to work to change and correct.

people mistreating people, especially the elderly, those with disabilities. Working hard.

What moves/grieves me? Somewhere in that is likely to be a clue to what God's given you a desire to heal.[64]

People not being passionate for God, even though often I am not.

What would I choose to do or be part of to bless someone else?

What am I good at? What strengths do I have?

You may know how you're gifted or you may doubt you are gifted at all. Right back in the womb, God carefully included everything in you that would become natural abilities. We get given different abilities and differing amounts of ability. God uses them to fulfil the jobs He has for us to do. Something I've noticed the devil making people feel guilty for is actually enjoying what they do. But God wants us to enjoy using the abilities He has given to us. Musical, artistic, domestic, athletic, academic, analytical, practical etc. etc. etc.

Singing. Public speaking- projection. Meeting people (but I can be shy), I'm good at list making.

What would I love to do if time and resources were unlimited?

Learn to be domestic, learn to lead worship; vocal, guitar & piano, dress to suit my shape, learn to be truly feminine, go on a long descipleship course- rooting myself firmly in Jesus.

What do I *really* want to be?

An on fire woman of God, who people feel like they meet Jesus when they meet me. Embracing my Godley femininty. Be ladylike but not boring & stale, firing others up & saying things how they are.

What are the most secret longings of my heart – the things I don't feel I could tell *anyone* because they're so big and daring?

To be a "Soul Survivor" style preacher. People looking up to me.

What should you do with your desires?

There is only one thing to do with your desires – share them with God. Be open with Him about what you yearn for. He can confirm and steer the longings or help you to see how what you think you want is being motivated by duty or fear or past pain and He has something better for you.

As you communicate with God about your desires, you will begin to co-labour and partner with Him. It's not robotic slavery but a friendship – participating with Jesus out of intimacy, dreaming and creating TOGETHER.

As you delight in God more and more and persistently look to Him to satisfy you, you'll get proper perspective on what you REALLY want.

> *Delight yourself also in the Lord, and He will give you the desires and secret petitions of your heart. Commit your way to the Lord – roll and repose [each care of] your road on Him; trust (lean on, rely on and be confident) also in Him, and He will bring it to pass.*
> (Psalm 37:4-5 AMP)

David Had A Dream!

David is an example of a man who delighted himself in the Lord. In 2Samuel 6, he celebrates God extravagantly, dancing before Him and worshipping. When his wife, Michal, criticised his behaviour, he didn't care. He said: *"In God's presence I'll dance all I want!… Oh yes, I'll dance to God's glory – more recklessly even than this. And as far as I'm concerned… I'll gladly look like a fool"* (2Samuel 6:22 MSG).

David valued His relationship with God above the opinions of any man. Taking delight in His Father mattered more than what anybody thought of him. It is out of that kind of friendship with God that pure desires and dreams come.

And David had a dream in his heart. He told God that he wanted the Ark, inhabited by God's presence, to be housed somewhere better than a tent (2Samuel 7). God responded by both increasing and confirming David's dream. God told David that He had a greater plan for David's own life that involved God continuing David's dynasty forever and that it would be David's son, Solomon, who would build a temple for God.

It was at the dedication of that temple that Solomon said: *"It was **in the heart** of David, my father, to build a house for the Name [the presence] of the Lord,* *the God of Israel."* (1Kings 8: 17 AMP)

David didn't ignore his desire or suppress it. His dream was big and bold but instead of him rejecting it as 'just him', his idea sparked a dialogue with God and God was able to unfold His vision for David's life.

20

Free To Have A Vision

Partners With Jesus

In this chapter we're going to be thinking more about how we can discover God's vision for our lives. But first of all, let's consider what Jesus' overall purpose actually is that we are called to play our unique part in.

Jesus came to Earth to *save that which was lost* (Matthew 18:11 AMP) — to reverse the effects of the fall and bring humanity back into friendship with God. Through Jesus, the goodness and power of God invaded this world that has turned away from its Creator. He quite simply brought Heaven to Earth. Everywhere He went, He replaced darkness and bondage with the joy, peace, wisdom, freedom and wholeness of Heaven.

Although Jesus has defeated the devil, he hasn't yet been finally subdued and until he is, demons still oppose the work of God's Kingdom. And that is where we come in — joining with Jesus in the work of ensuring that God's Kingdom is built on the Earth, allowing His Spirit in us to bring Heaven to Earth everywhere we go, revealing the glory and goodness of God to a world crying out for truth.

Now Jesus is seated in Heaven with authority over everything (Ephesians 1:20-21) and **the incredible thing is that He shares His throne with us!** (Ephesians 2:6).

You Rule!

As King, Jesus rules. As Priest, He prays God's will into being. Jesus has *formed us into a kingdom (a royal race), priests to His God and Father* (Revelation 1:5-6 AMP).

We reign and rule with Him as we know God's will in a situation and command the Earth's circumstance to line up with the will of Heaven. This is the most exciting privilege. Rather than just making surface changes on the face of this planet as we pour money and time into projects, as believers, we can do so much more! We can discover the will of Heaven in a situation and pray that it will be done. We can ask God to reveal what dark forces are behind the problem and command them to leave in Jesus' name. We can seek God for a verse from the Bible to speak into the situation and stand on in faith.

Discovering God's Vision For Your Life

Part of the way God shows us His plan for our lives is through revealing the desires planted in our hearts. And we've seen that we need to take the things we think we want seriously and share them with God.

Here is my guide for the rest of discovering and fulfilling God's vision for your life:

1. Get Into Position
That's what Habakkuk did:

> *I will [in my thinking] stand upon my post of observation and station myself on the tower or fortress, and will watch to see what He will say within me.*
>
> (Habakkuk 2:1 AMP)

And we need to do the same – to be quiet before God in the place of prayer and intimacy rather than running busily around. Then you can ask Him:

"Lord, who is ___Rachael_____? Who have you made me to
(insert your name here)
be? What's my life for?"

FASTING

You may want to consider fasting to bring greater clarity to your praying, denying your flesh to draw as close as possible to God's heart. That's what Ezra did to receive direction:

> *I proclaimed a fast there, at the river of Ahava, that we might humble ourselves before our God **to seek of Him a straight and right way** for us, our little ones and all our possessions.*
> (Ezra 8:21 AMP)

Fasting was a regular part of the life of the early church, reflecting Jesus' teaching. He made it clear that He would expect us to fast – He says *when* and not 'if' we fast (Matthew 6:17-18 AMP).

How you fast, from what, for how long, when and for what is between you and God. Personally, up to this point in my life, I have been led to fast for a day a week – that has been from one meal or something else, not food (like television). Putting that day aside to pray in detail for whatever matters God is laying on my heart brings focus to my week. I have also taken periods of a week or a month where I have gone without something and committed to extra prayer time for a certain matter.

Has it brought clarity to my prayer time? Movement in situations? Without fail. Is what I do the best way? No. It is GOD's way for ME. The when, the how and the what for are all *completely* directed by God and that is the key.

2. And Expect An Answer

Habakkuk was in no doubt that God would answer and we need to be the same. Believe that God wants you to fulfill His plans, and that He wants you to know how to. Have your Bible and pen and paper ready and expect Him to speak.

3. Be Open To What God Has To Say

When God tells us about who we are and what He wants us to do, it can be quite shocking because He speaks to our potential. He speaks to the princess in us. Gideon and Mary are two people in the Bible who God told of His enormous plans for their lives. He addressed the prince in Gideon, (a man who felt anything but strong): *"mighty man of valour"* (Judges 6:12 NKJV) and the princess in Mary, (a girl who called herself simply a *handmaiden* (Luke 1:38 AMP)): *"blessed... before all other women"* (Luke 1:28 AMP).

God sees us differently to the way that we have most likely grown up seeing ourselves so don't show false humility when He speaks to your potential. *The Message* Bible paraphrases Gabriel's greeting to Mary: *"Good morning! You're beautiful with God's beauty, beautiful inside and out!"* (Luke 1:28 MSG). Value each and every one of those "Good morning, beautiful" moments.

Be aware that the vision for your life is not just about finding the right career. Obviously if you have a job, God has a plan for you to do the right one but although we're used to a person's job being their identity, that's not how God values and defines us.

4. Write It Down

> *And the Lord answered me and said,* **Write the vision**.
> (Habakkuk 2:2 AMP)

As God speaks, keep a note of it. Over time, as the picture becomes clearer, review the material. You may break it into sections and add God's strategies for its fulfilment as He shares them with you.

5. Talk To God About What You Hear

We can begin to have some idea of what is in our hearts to do, the dreams placed there by God and hear God's whispers beginning to reveal His purposes. It may be that desires surface, you have pictures, God brings verses to your attention or He seems to be saying things in other ways. These are what I think of as the 'glimmers'.

I spent far too much of my life completely stressed off my head about finding out what God wanted me to do. I got absolutely nowhere but as I got to know God better, there were glimmers emerging – ideas about the kind of person I had been made to be, the direction that God wanted my life to take. The problem was that I didn't really know what to do with them.

I looked ahead and couldn't see how the vague sketch that I had of a vision for the kind of work God wanted me to do could possibly happen. I didn't have the money to put it into play and I couldn't see how I would ever get any money from going with it. And indeed, I did go through rather a prolonged patch where I gave up everything to do God's will and didn't seem to get *anything* in return. I could hear all the voices that said: "It's so irresponsible, so lacking in common sense, so downright stupid to follow God."

There was still a lot of uncertainty in me about how to do what He wanted or even exactly what He did want. I was terrified by that lack of knowledge and would try to make my own strategies rather than trusting God to provide a plan. I felt really guilty at the thought of doing what God wanted me to do because it was actually what *I* wanted to do. It seemed so lazy to spend my life doing what I enjoyed. I felt embarrassed too, to be following some half formed dream when it was something that other people wouldn't think I was worthy of or capable enough for.

Ask God about the glimmers. Are they definitely from Him? Are the desires stirring in you stirring because you've been praying for direction and it's the way God is answering? Are the Bible verses that keep coming up, or a sermon that seemed to speak so directly to you, God trying to show you His dreams for your life? Keep talking to Him.

6. **Don't Let Unbelief Or Distrust Make You Waver** (Romans 4:20 AMP)

If the glimmers are seeds of the vision, you need to BELIEVE what God is saying and AGREE that you desire His will to be done, that you see it as a blessing. Mary could have gone crazy when she was told that she, an unmarried woman, was going to become pregnant with the Son of God. Instead, she said: *"Let it be done to me according to what you have said"* (Luke 1:38 AMP).

> And *Blessed (happy, to be envied) is she who* **believed** *that there would be a fulfilment of the things that were spoken to her from the Lord.*
>
> (Luke 1:45 AMP)

Abraham had no earthly reason, when he looked at his circumstances, to believe God that he was going to be the father of many nations but *He did not weaken in faith when he considered the [utter]* **impotence** *of his own body, which was as good as dead because he was about a hundred years old, or [when he* *considered] the **barrenness** of Sarah's [deadened] womb* (Romans 4:19 AMP).

It can take time to find out what you were made for, what God wants you to do. If you are waiting for God to make clear how the glimmers shape into a vision and for a strategy for its fulfilment, pray that when the clear vision does come, when God tells you about the amazing things you can bring forth with your life, by His Spirit, and it all sounds impossible, that He will help you respond in faith and expectation. We'll be talking more about this in the next couple of chapters but know that you are able because God is able and with you. Don't allow past failure, present challenges or fears for the future steal what God is promising.

7. Don't Let Other People Influence You Negatively

Paul kept the news of his calling to himself. He waited on God. He didn't ask other people's opinions, not even men of experience and wisdom in the things of God. As he says: *"I did not confer with flesh and blood"* (Galatians 1:16 AMP). Over three years later, when he began operating in his calling, people recognised that it was indeed from God.

When I tentatively mentioned to someone what I thought was the vision God had given to me, they said: "That's not the kind of thing that makes a vision." That really threw me at the time, but God has confirmed it too many times since then for me to doubt it anymore. I'm certainly not telling you not to speak to anybody about what God seems to be saying to you, just warning you to seek Him for wisdom about whom, if anyone, you should tell.

8. Pray And Speak Your Vision Into Being

God *speaks of the non-existent things that [He has foretold and promised] as if they [already] existed* (Romans 4:17 AMP). You need to do the same – to see things the way God has declared they will be and pray and declare in faith that they will indeed be so.

> *No unbelief or distrust made him waver (doubtingly question)*
> *concerning the promise of God, but he grew strong and was*
> ***empowered by faith as he gave praise and glory to God,***
> *fully satisfied and assured that God was able and mighty to keep His*
> *word and to do what He had promised.*
> (Romans 4:20-21 AMP)

9.Don't Be A Quitter And Lose Out (Hebrews 10:39 MSG)

The last thing to say is quite simply: Don't give up! Seeing your vision through will require patience but it will be worth it.

> *For the vision is yet for an appointed time and it hastens to the end [fulfilment]; it will not deceive or disappoint. Though it tarry, wait [earnestly] for it, because it will surely come;* ***it will not be behindhand on its appointed day.***
>
> (Habakkuk 2:3 AMP)

> *You have need of steadfast patience and endurance, so that you may perform and fully accomplish the will of God, and thus receive and* ***carry away [and enjoy to the full] what is promised.***
>
> (Hebrews 10:36 AMP)

21

Free To Be Able

Who am I to...?

If you find yourself responding to the glimmers like I did: "That's impossible!" "There's no way I could ever...!" "But who am I to do this?", you will be encouraged to know that we're not the first people to feel like that!

God famously spoke to Moses from the burning bush and told him that He had a *huge* plan for Moses' life – to lead God's people out of Egypt. Moses' response was: *"WHO AM I, that I should go to Pharaoh and bring the Israelites out of Egypt?"* (Exodus 3:11 AMP). God had big plans for Gideon too. But like Moses, Gideon asked: *"Oh Lord, how can I deliver Israel? Behold, my clan is the poorest in Manasseh, and I am the least in my father's house"* (Judges 6:15 AMP). But God said to Moses: *"I will surely be with you"* (Exodus 3:12 AMP), and to Gideon: *"Surely I will be with you"* (Judges 6:16 AMP).

Both men were really saying to God: "Who am I to do what you have planned for me to do?" And it was as if He was saying in reply: "You, Moses. You Gideon. You are the men I will go with."

It is as if He is saying to our:

> "But who am I to do your will, to do what you have planned? It's all too good to be true. I can't be that privileged surely. Everyone's going to think I'm mad! And what about money? And what exactly am I going to *do* – how will it work?"

> *"Before I formed you,* <u>Rachael</u> *, in the womb*
> (insert your name here)
> *I knew [and] approved of you [as My chosen instrument], and before*

you were born I separated and set you apart,... [and] I appointed you (Jeremiah 1:5 AMP) **and I will be with you** to work my plan through."

'We ask ourselves – who am I to be brilliant, beautiful, talented and fabulous? Actually, who are you not to be! You are a child of God. Your playing small does not serve the world. We were born to make manifest the glory of God that is within us.'

– Marianne Williamson

She is...

Read this description of the woman described in Proverbs 31 (AMP):

*A **capable, intelligent** and **virtuous** woman, who is he who can find her? **She is far more precious than jewels**, and **her value is far above rubies or pearls.** The heart of her husband trusts in her confidently and relies on and believes in her safely, so that he has no lack of honest gain or need of dishonest spoil. She will comfort, encourage and do him only good as long as there is life within her.*

*She seeks out the wool and flax and **works with willing hands** to develop it. She is like the merchant ships loaded with foodstuffs, she brings her household's food from a far [country]. She rises while yet it is night and **gets spiritual food for her household** and assigns her maids their tasks.*

*She considers a new field before she buys or accepts it – **expanding prudently** [and not courting neglect of her present duties by assuming others]. With her savings [of time and strength] **she plants fruitful vines** in her vineyard.*

She girds herself with strength *[spiritual, mental, and physical fitness for her God-given task] and makes her arms strong and firm. She tastes and sees that her gain from work [with and for God] is good; **her lamp goes not out;** but it burns on continually through the night [of trouble, privation or sorrow, warning away fear, doubt and distrust]. She lays her hands to the spindle, and her hands hold the distaff.*

She opens her hand to the poor; *yes,* ***she reaches out her filled hands***

to the needy [whether in body, mind or spirit]. **She fears not** the snow for her family, for all her household are doubly clothed in scarlet. She makes for herself coverlets, cushions and rugs of tapestry.

Her clothing is of linen, pure white and fine, and of purple [such as that of which the clothing of the priests and the hallowed cloths of the temple are made]. Her husband is known in the city's gates, when he sits among the elders of the land. She makes fine linen garments and leads others to buy them; she delivers to the merchants girdles [or sashes that free one for service]. Strength and dignity are her clothing and her position is strong and secure.

She rejoices over the future – the latter day or time to come [knowing that she and her family are in readiness for it]! She opens her mouth with skilful and godly Wisdom, and **in her tongue is the law of kindness** – giving counsel and instruction. She looks well to how things go in her household, and **the bread of idleness [gossip, discontent and self-pity] she will not eat.**

Her children rise up and call her **blessed [happy, fortunate and to be envied];** and her husband boasts of and praises her, saying, "Many daughters have done virtuously, nobly and well [with the strength of character that is steadfast in goodness] but you excel them all. Charm and grace are deceptive, and beauty is vain [because it is not lasting], but **a woman who reverently and worshipfully fears the Lord,** she shall be praised! Give her of the fruit of her hands, and let her own works praise her in the gates of the city!"

Rachael   **is...**

(insert your name here)

Now write your own description of how you would like to be described. This may help you further discover the vision God has placed in your heart for what He would like to see happen in your life:

Who Is She?!

There is no doubt that the Proverbs 31 woman is remarkable! Just think of being a woman who is that capable of navigating her way through the life she has been given. Does she make you feel intimidated – some kind of model of perfection that you could never be?

The Proverbs 31 woman's husband says that she surpasses all Superwomen! What makes her so worthy of praise in comparison to other women is her *reverent and worshipful fear of the Lord*. It sets her apart and above and equips and empowers her. This is *the beginning and the principal ... part of Wisdom* (Proverbs 1:7 AMP) that permeates every area of her life. This reverent and worshipful fear of God is our *treasure* and His (Isaiah 33:6 AMP). A person like this God *will teach in the way that* they *should choose*, they will *dwell at ease* and know the *secret [of the sweet, satisfying companionship] of the Lord* (Psalm 25:12-14 AMP).

What is a reverent and worshipful fear of the Lord? A humble heart towards God that lays down niggling doubt. FEAR OF THE LORD says: "I'll trust you, I'll believe what you say, I'll submit to you – to follow you, to obey you, to walk humbly with you. At every turn I'll praise you and declare that you are good. I'm choosing to lean on your Holy Spirit to do everything for, in and through me."

"I Can Because God Can"

I believe the Proverbs woman shouldn't intimidate us but be a huge encouragement. It's inspiring to think that this kind of potential is within ALL women filled and empowered by the Holy Spirit. I like to think of her as an "I can because God can" woman which is actually the sort of woman all of us can be! When you read the way you'd like to be described, do you think of a day far off when you may be able to be that person? If you are a woman redeemed by Jesus' blood, reborn with a beautiful spirit and filled with the Spirit of the Living God, whatever has gone before, whatever healing you are still receiving and requiring from God, you can begin to be that woman TODAY!

Jesus told His disciples that they would be better off when He ascended to heaven and the Holy Spirit came. And in Acts we see their resulting supernatural lives – supernatural praying, preaching, guidance, protection. It is the same Spirit of God who lives in us. The Holy Spirit has everything you need to live the life God has called you to.

When we say we're unable to do what we feel God is calling us to do we are saying that God can't do it either which is not true. He is more than able to do anything through you. You have got to look beyond what you can see with your human eyes and start to see through eyes of faith. As Paul said:

> *I can do all things **through** Christ who strengthens me.*
> (Philippians 4:13 NKJV)

What's more, we can do nothing that has any value in our own strength:

> *I am the vine, you are the branches; he who abides in Me, and I in him, he bears much fruit; for apart from Me you can do **nothing.***
> (John 15:5 NKJV)

the holy spirit:

Comforter · Counsellor · Helper · Advocate · Intercessor · Strengthener · Standby · to be in close fellowship with you · Spirit of Truth · will guide you into the whole, full Truth · He will tell whatever He hears [from the Father] · He will announce and declare to you the things that will happen in the future · He will honour and glorify Me [Jesus], because He will take of what is Mine and will reveal it to you (From John 16:7-15 AMP) · Spirit of wisdom and understanding · Spirit of counsel and might · Spirit of knowledge and of the reverential and obedient fear of the Lord (Isaiah 11:2 AMP)

Following His Lead

It really does only rest on a CHOICE, an act of your will, whether you are going to decide to live in the power of the Holy Spirit, yielded to His presence within, so that He can overflow from you. Will you begin to listen to the internal promptings of the Holy Spirit, His whispering and nudging in your heart? Will you begin to pay a lot more attention to your instinct and gut feeling?

We are made and empowered to live in the Spirit, to speak God's words and do what He wants us to do. The Holy Spirit is one with your spirit and if you are living sensitive to Him, you will begin to notice that your spirit speaks to you much more quickly than your mind. Before your mind understands, your spirit already says "yes" or "no" which is what we call our intuition. For example, you may be about to criticise someone and before your mind is ready to form the words, you sense the Spirit saying: "Don't say it."

Recently I bought something to wear that didn't fit properly. It was expensive and because I had cut out the label, I couldn't get a refund. There was a whisper inside me that said: "Just give it away." But I didn't pay full attention to that whisper and actually say to the Spirit: "Am I hearing right, is that really what you want me to do, who should I give it to?" Instead, I rushed to try to change it – there were just a few days where I could have an exchange and vouchers for the rest of the money. I couldn't find anything to change it for although I was praying to find the right thing.

In the end I gave up and I remembered that whisper. I asked God who I should give it to and trusted Him that it was something He wanted them to have. Ignoring the Spirit in the first place was the kind of disobedience it is very easy to fall into especially if we allow ourselves to live in a state of strain or stress. It is far easier to be led by God when we're not frustrated or anxious but have an inner rest and peace.

Calm

So, if you want to be led by the Holy Spirit, calm down! You can face each situation in life in one of two ways. You can react in the flesh by being afraid/ violent/ swearing/ churning thoughts around in your mind/ being negative/ running straight to a book, someone's opinion or the internet/ having a tantrum/ being impatient/ depressed/ discouraged/ grumbling/ complaining and self pitying. Or you can first turn inwards to the Spirit and listen to His guidance in the situation. Like that, you can live reliant on the daily leading of the inner voice of Jesus.

Quick

When you hear the Spirit's voice, obey it. When He tells you to encourage someone with a specific verse from the Bible for instance, just do it. It's so easy to put off doing something like that because you reason with your mind that it's a really bad idea. You need to begin to become more concerned with whether you bear witness with something in your spirit than with checking in with your over active mind. If you are willing to make the odd mistake and to get going, you will increasingly walk in the will of God as Jesus leads you through His Spirit within.

Confident

It means forgetting about public opinion – forgetting the 'they' who have told us what we should wear, eat and do; who've defined a hierarchy of professions, places to live, people to know. It means that if you feel led to do something, you do it. If something isn't right for you, you don't do it. It doesn't matter what other people think. Your only responsibility is to be what God has created you to be. Other people's opinions aren't your problem.

So how do we know we're being led by the Spirit?

* We will be led in wisdom and moderation unlike when we are led by fear which always operates in extremes.
* We will not be told to do anything that is against what it says in the Bible.
* We'll desire to please God.

- Whatever we do will honour and glorify God. We'll be able to worship God while we do it.
- We'll have freedom.
- We'll produce the fruit of the Spirit, the very character of Jesus – *love, joy, peace, patience, kindness, goodness, faithfulness, gentleness, self-control* (Galatians 5:22-23 NIV).

> 'Living from our hearts is not simply doing what our feelings tell us. That would be folly. Living from our hearts means that there is an inner directive that, if governed by the Spirit of God, keeps us on a path that is spiritually attuned to who we are and how God is leading.'
>
> – Friesen[65]

Relying On His Power

You've been created to be amazing on this earth. Amazing in every role God has called you to, be that mother, wife, friend, church member, colleague, career woman, disciple, homemaker… And you really do have the potential and capacity in Christ to radiate God's glory always. To be an attractive, soothing presence. To transmit peace in the midst of a crisis situation. To be a great friend. To be confident, capable, competent. To achieve. To remain a delight whatever the challenges! To have answers that display God's wisdom. To make a difference to this world. To be nothing less than an encounter with Jesus.

None of this has anything to with background, education, or your own strength or abilities. This is simply because you are occupied by God. The normal atmosphere of walking in the Spirit is praise and thanksgiving, it's overflowing joy and peace. It's being given abundant love for people you couldn't otherwise conceive of loving. It's changing the atmosphere around you. It can be horrible but in Christ, you can be surrounded by an irresistible aroma:

> *Thanks be to God, who in Christ always leads us in triumph [as trophies of Christ's victory] and through us spreads and makes evident the **FRAGRANCE** of the knowledge of God everywhere.*
> (2Corinthians 2:14 AMP)

Take It And Use It

As you ask for help from the Holy Spirit, begin to take it: "Lord, I need your power/ love/ joy/ hope/ wisdom for this situation and thank you that I take it and rely on it now."

What you take you've got!

Jesus was busy but He didn't burn out because He only did His Father's will (John 5:19). He promised that His yoke is easy and burden light when we work with Him (Matthew 11:28-30) and that it's actually our *food* to do His will (John 4:34). Food is strengthening and enjoyable – it doesn't make us weak and exhausted. Like so many people do, we'll burn out if we work in our own power but if we wait on the Lord, we will be like an eagle (Isaiah 40:30-31) which soars on the wind without using its own energy. We will walk and run in the energy of the Holy Spirit and know what it is to have our work invigorated and our speech enlivened! (2 Thessalonians 2:16-17).

See Yourself Full

You have got to begin to see yourself full of God. A woman:

> *Who, by (in consequence of) the [action of His] power that is at work within us, is able to [carry out His purpose and] do superabundantly, far over and above all that we [dare] ask or think [infinitely beyond our highest prayers, desires, thoughts, hopes, or dreams].*
> (Ephesians 3:20 AMP)

When we're reborn, the spiritual gifts God has given to us come to life inside us.

GIFTS ARE LISTED IN ROMANS
Proclamation/Prophecy: Hearing a message from God that He wants you to speak to an individual or group.
Serving: Seeing and doing jobs that need to be done.
Teaching: Communicating biblical information so others can understand

it and grow in their knowledge of God.

Encouragement/Exhortation: Speaking a word of encouragement or advice that inspires someone's faith.

Giving: Giving what you have to others.

Leadership: Seeing God's vision, finding His strategy to complete it and guiding others, who He wants involved, to make it happen.

Mercy: Being moved by the way others are feeling and showing kindness that brings blessing and relief.

GIFTS ARE LISTED IN 1 CORINTHIANS

Wisdom: Knowing and presenting God's mind on a matter.

Knowledge: To receive information from the Spirit, about a person or situation, you wouldn't naturally know, to bring encouragement or direction to somebody.

Faith: Having a complete and unshakeable belief and trust in what God says He will do.

Healing: Praying for sick people and seeing God make them well and whole.

Miracles: Being the channel God performs acts of power through.

Discernment: Knowing whether something is of God or the devil.

Speaking In A Spiritual Language: Delivering a message in a language you have never learned.

Interpreting A Spiritual Language: Delivering the translation of a message given in tongues.

Helps: Working behind the scenes to support someone's ministry.

Administration: Organising practical things that need doing.

GIFTS ARE LISTED IN EPHESIANS:

Apostle: Creating new situations to gather people together like a new church or Bible study or group.

Evangelist: Sharing the truth with non believers.

Pastor/Shepherd: Caring for believers and providing spiritual food.

Prophet: Defined above under 'Prophecy'.

Teacher: Defined above under 'Teaching'.

Celibacy (1Corinthians 7:7-8) Remaining single to fulfil God's purposes.

Hospitality (1Peter 4:9) Opening your home and making people feel welcome.

Intercession (Colossians 1:9) Praying for people and situations.

Just because you have never done these things doesn't mean that you can't or aren't made to. The Holy Spirit is within you and the gifts describe the way He operates so are available within you – they depend on God's ability and not our own.

God has a lot for us to do and to ensure it is possible for everything to get done, He has given these gifts to us in differing quantities. Read the list and why not begin by asking yourself which of these things you would love to do! I remember finding out about spiritual gifts and doing a quiz where you had to answer questions about what you were good at and from that the quiz told you what your gifts were. When I looked at the results, they were exactly what I would have loved my gifts to be. Before that I had imagined other people would say I was too immature in the things of God to have those gifts and it would have been arrogant to own them.

Never mind how you will be called to use them, just ask yourself which of those gifts above you'd love to describe what you may be called to do. Then chat to Jesus about it. Ask Him: "Is that really me?! Is that really some of how we're going to partner together?" Start praying for opportunities to develop and use your gifts.

In case you are doubtful, it is not pride to discover what gifts God wants to develop in you. It is His will for you, vital to you participating with Jesus.

22

Free To Succeed

The Old Shame Thing

This fallen world has told us what success is. It varies depending on the culture, background and generation we grow up in. But on the whole it's seen to be about outstanding achievement at school and in a career; a lot of money; fabulous property; an equally 'successful' husband, friends and dynasty of children and grandchildren; a slim body and unlined skin.

It's all the things that we seek to overcome our feelings of shame, relying on them to speak of our value.

When we become friends with God, we often transfer our worldly definitions of success to a new arena. Again it varies but it's often about belonging to the 'right' church; which of the big names you know; how many people you can convert; how many prayers you get 'answered'; being in demand for having lots of money to give away; for leading amazing worship or doing miracles. Or we can discover some of what it is God wants us to do on this earth, and before we know it, our identity has become our vision and calling – this new job description.

Redefining Success

But we're missing God's perspective. In order to fulfill all we have been made for, we need our minds renewed to clearly see what success is from God's point of view. We are successful because of JESUS! Invited to be the intimate companion of the King of Kings, to participate with the God of everything for His will to be done on the Earth.

This is success but it's not for anything that we have ever done. It is all because of what Jesus has done for us. What He has made available to all mankind.

Jesus is the highest reward we will ever receive! His love, His sacrifice, Himself! Financial, social, career or even ministry 'success' can't be our primary life's reward. They can't be the things that define our value. You are the daughter God adores and died for. You have accepted what Jesus has done for you and become a lover of God. That makes you eternally successful and eternally significant! When Jesus is our all, we find purpose, pleasure and success. Our foremost identity is to be loved by Him and to be a lover of Him.

You'll **always** be successful if loving Him and being loved by Him is your primary reward and concern. When Jesus was asked what we should do to carry out what God requires, He replied that we need only believe in Him:
"This the work (service) that God asks of you: that you believe in the One (Jesus) *Whom He has sent [that you cleave to, trust, rely on, and have faith in His Messenger]"* (John 6:29 AMP).

You are not and never will be a failure because of God's commitment to you. The whole point of what Jesus has done is to stop you being a failure every time you get it wrong. Your flesh may be weak, you may stumble at times but God's love will not let you go.

You May Be Fooled to Walk in Failure

In spite of the fact we are a great success in God's eyes, we can still feel like a failure. And feeling like a failure is absolutely horrible. You can make great attempts, putting your near best in to things time and again but get nothing out. It can seem as if you're always impotent, always barren, that your efforts are always futile, and as if that's the way it will always be. Hurt, bewildered and angry, it makes you feel as if you've been trampled and thrown in a bin. Your identity: 'pointless failure'. But God has a great word of encouragement for those of us who have felt like that:

"I have chosen you and will not throw you away."
(Isaiah 41:9 NLT)

If you have known failure and have what feels like a pattern of things messing up on you, you can quickly find you've taken **'fool and failure'** on as your identity. That's just the way the devil wants it. He never wanted us to begin to uncover God's plans for our lives and when we do start to discover the dreams in our hearts, he'd like us to give them up as hopeless. He wants us to feel that once a failure, always a failure.

But the past doesn't have to dictate your future. Just because you have ended up a long way from where you're beginning to see that you could be doesn't mean that you're doomed to a life of compromise. Quite the opposite in fact!

I used to fear the past had stolen my future and God spoke into my heart: "I have a plan. It's what I made you for. Nothing that has happened is going to steal it. You live half a life sometimes… thinking that you're only going to have half a destiny, only going to be half used because of the way things have been. You've heard lies about what you 'deserve'… You think in terms of concession, compromise, only being half a person. You are the way I made you to be – forgiven, restored, indwelt, empowered… You are seen. You are adored. You are purposed. I want you to enter into the fullness of yourself and your life."

You can still live in God's plans for your life and you can trust Him to turn the things that have happened around for good! Look at Joseph. His brothers were determined to ruin his destiny. He was in prison for years for something he didn't even do. But Joseph didn't give in and label himself a 'fool and failure'. He stayed strong in God and God prospered him. God saved his life, got him out of prison and made him a great ruler.

Begin to confess Ephesians 2:10, that you are living in God's good plan, that you're on track:

"*I am recreated in Christ Jesus that I may do those good works which God predestined (planned beforehand) for me (taking paths which He prepared ahead of time) that I should walk in them (living the good life which He prearranged and made ready for me to live).*"

(AMP)

The past doesn't have to mean the future's only going to be a dim version of what it could have been. The future's God's and He has good plans.

Disappointment may have been a key enemy tactic to destroy your potential, and calling but be sure, there is no onslaught God's power can't defeat and overcome. There is an impact for you to have for His glory on this earth and none of the seemingly insurmountable odds are insurmountable to Him. In the power of the Holy Spirit, you can rise up and go beyond the things that seek to hold you back.

Warrior Princess

In The Barren Place...

Perhaps you are in the barren place where the ground seems unyielding. You're claiming God's promises of provision and breakthrough but you're still waiting to see the manifestation of all the good things He is doing on your behalf. Or maybe you're waiting for what seems like forever for Him to give you a clear vision for your life.

At a time like that, the devil tries to keep your eyes down on your circumstances, to put on you the humiliation of being poor or friendless or jobless or childless or alone or physically weak; that choosing life with God was stupid and by worldly standards, you are a nobody.

But if you are willing, barren can be your doorway to living in the reality of being free from shame, to really being you. Barren removes status symbols – those things you have relied on to speak for you about your identity and value. When you don't step out on the arm of Mr Rich and Sexy anymore, you don't have lovely clothes anymore, you don't have that job anymore, you haven't got the club membership anymore, you don't have that car anymore, that group of people don't want to know you anymore, you're not interesting for what you were interesting for anymore, then you step out as you. Just YOU!

And you choose then whether you will walk in the old shame and feelings of worthlessness or whether you will live out the truth. I have crumpled up in the barren place, facing my inability to save myself. Unable to make myself succeed, unable to save the lives of my family, unable to get myself out of debt, unable to heal my own body, unable to control the future.

And I have discovered the true status symbol – the only thing that gives me any value is Jesus.

> *We...* **exult and glory and pride ourselves in Jesus Christ,** *and put no confidence or dependence [on what we are] in the flesh and on outward privileges and physical advantages and external appearances...* **I count everything as loss (mere rubbish (refuse dregs)** (Philippians 3:8 AMP)) *compared to the possession of the* **priceless privilege** *(the overwhelming preciousness, the surpassing worth, and supreme advantage) of knowing Jesus... and of progressively becoming more deeply and intimately acquainted with Him.*
> (Philippians 3:3, 8 AMP)

Having crumpled up, I know that it is possible, however low your circumstances are trying to keep you, to stand up from the heap that you are in. Whatever you may be going through, God is good and if you let Him, He will bring good out of where you are. A barren time can become an opportunity to grow – to ask God what he wants to reveal to us about Himself, and ourselves, through it. Here's how you can play your part and rise up in the place of barrenness and uncertainty:

Check In With God

If you don't feel you're enjoying a blessed, abundant life then you need to check in with God: "Is it an attitude in me/ something I'm doing/ or not doing/ some external force I need to pray against that is blocking blessing in my life?" If it is, He will show you so you can put it right in the power of His Spirit.

Decide That Barrenness Will Not Beat You

God is good all the time but sometimes we can seriously wonder! The things He says in the Bible don't look like they're true and our grief can begin to separate us from Him. Barren will try to make you bitter against God, life, others, everything, which is ugly, horrible and destructive. We can't allow anything – no amount of waiting for God to act or questions that we don't have answers to – to interrupt our companionship with Him. Keeping the relationship lines open with God truly is your lifeline. *Be zealous to know the Lord [to appreciate, give heed to, and cherish Him]* (Hosea 6:3 AMP) whatever is going on in your life.

Fall Deeper In Love With God

If you let it, the barren place can actually establish your focus on God. You discover God really is enough, that in the absence of just about everything else you've regarded as essential to your wellbeing, you are happy and fulfilled in the depths of your being. You see what 'really living,' having the 'real deal' and being 'blessed' are all about.

Waking up each day to be loved by God really is enough.

> *As for me..., I shall be **fully satisfied,** when I awake [to find myself] beholding Your form [and having sweet communion with You].*
> (Psalm 17:15 AMP)

Praise Him

As you fix your eyes on God and the possibilities that lie in Him rather than feeling down when you look at your circumstances, you just have to praise Him!

> *Though the fig tree does **not blossom** and there is **no fruit** on the vines, [though] the product of **the olive fails** and the fields **yield no food,** though the **flock is cut off** from the fold and there are **no cattle** in the stalls, **yet I will rejoice** in the Lord; I will exult in the [victorious] God of my salvation! The Lord God is my Strength, my personal bravery, and my invincible army; He makes my feet like hinds' feet and will make me to walk [not to stand still in terror, but to walk] and make [spiritual] **progress upon my high places [of trouble, suffering, or responsibility]!***
> (Habakkuk 3:17-19 AMP)

> *Blessed are the people who know the passwords of praise,*
> *Who shout on parade in the bright presence of God.*
> *Delighted, they dance all day long; they know*

Who you are, what you do — they can't keep it quiet!
(Psalm 89:35 MSG)

Fall In Love With Life

If you let it, the barren place will give you a new perspective on life that will give you a deeper peace than you have known. It offers to free your mind from worldly conventional thinking, make you more relaxed and generous hearted. You start to appreciate things you took for granted before. You become grateful for plain everything. Life becomes precious as you discover new and simple pleasures.

You find that you see each day as special for no other reason than that it was made by God:

This is the day which the Lord has brought about; we will rejoice and be glad in it.
(Psalm 118:24 AMP)

Enjoy Yourself!

Sometimes it seems as if we just live to finish things, to get to the next destination, that everything is a means to an end. Living like that, we miss out on enjoying things along the way. The world says slow is failure, speed is success. In the barren place, you discover that God doesn't always move quickly, that healing can be a very slow, gentle process.

*All the days of the desponding and afflicted are made evil [by anxious thoughts and forebodings], but **He who has a glad heart has a continual feast [regardless of circumstances].***
(Proverbs 15:15 AMP)

See Who You Really Are

I truly know that it is hard to believe you have any worth when you seemingly have no identity or anything to offer but your physical presence. But whatever has brought you into this place, you have been, are and will be significant. You have to become convinced of your value – your essentialness – because God is! It is truly infinite.

> *The Lord has chosen you to be His **treasured possession.***
> (Deuteronomy 14:2 NIV)

Your value doesn't alter however mundane life seems. As part of God's will for you at this time, what feel like no more than fragments – joining with prayers and worship in church, yet another day of filing for an ungrateful boss, being present in the supermarket – matter. You have a part to play in what Jesus wants to do on this Earth whether everyone else likes it or not. You may feel people look at you and just see a bit of dust but you're of as much value as they are:

> *You belong here, with as much right to the name Christian as anyone...*
> *He's using us all – irrespective of how we got here – in what He is building. He used the apostles and prophets for the foundation. Now He's using **you.***
> (Ephesians 3:20-21 MSG)

I love the way the Proverbs 31 woman is described as being like a merchant ship loaded with foodstuffs, that she brings her household's food from a far country. It suggests that what she brings to the people around her is precious, exotic things they couldn't get locally or from anyone else. She brings what is needed and will nourish them. That speaks of far more than giving people food to eat but of giving them a smile, a word of love and encouragement, **the dynamic that you alone can bring to their lives.** Don't allow anyone to make you feel guilty for your presence on this earth – you have a lot to give. It is time to acknowledge it – that you are beautiful, simply exquisite and precious.

See Your Potential

You are a woman with great potential. There is always more for you to give, even when you feel spent, because Jesus is within you and there is always more treasure, more seeds of greatness, for Him to unearth. You are full of limitless, unending possibilities.

In God there is no limit. It is time to think, talk, love, act, give, help, dream bigger. There is a very big future ahead, an eternal future. That means endless capacities. You were born to no less than display the glory and goodness of God within you.

Fall In Love With Humanity

In the barren place, you nurse your wounds. You have nothing left to give except yourself and you find that not everyone sticks around when you can no longer give them what they liked you for. **Because you're not, you realise how desperately you want to be liked for being you.** That's how God likes you and more than ever you see that's how He wants you to like Him, how He wants you to like yourself.

You start to get what Jesus means about loving others the way He loves you and the way you love yourself (John 13:34). You realise that you have got to begin to see yourself and love yourself the way God does before you can successfully love anybody else.

God is passionately in love with humanity and in the barren place, you find yourself falling in love with what God loves the way He loves it. You thank God for the way others have hurt you, repent that you haven't loved them properly at all and pray that you will learn never to love them wrong again. You become determined to stop being the devil's advocate and start being the Holy Spirit's, helping and not obstructing the work God wants to do in their lives. You desire:

- To treat others like they're God's treasures.
- To show them what it's like to be loved freely and lavishly, not measuring their value against the world's standards.
- To love them just for who they are – nothing to do with what they can do for you/ give you. Not...
  - because knowing them helps you feel better about yourself by

putting them down.

- because knowing them will raise your status by being associated with them.

- to boss them around and try to make them what you want them to be, what you think is good.

- to allow fear to make you wrap them in cotton wool but allow them to live.

• To always have the RIGHT thing to say that will speak words of life and blessing to their potential.

Don't Lose Sight Of The Bigger Purpose

> *For the teraphim (household idols) have spoken vanity (emptiness, falsity, and futility) and the diviners have seen a lie and the dreamers have told false dreams; they comfort in vain. Therefore the people go their way like sheep; they are afflicted and hurt because there is no shepherd.*
>
> (Zechariah 10:2 AMP)

God's big purpose? That *no one* should perish (2Peter 3:9). As you fall in love with God and His world, you want everyone to know that they do have a shepherd and don't have to live an empty, futile life anymore.

You may not know exactly what your personal role in God's purposes is yet. But you can be sure that everyday a person crosses your path, there is someone to love with God's love.

> *He has given us 'the ministry of reconciliation [that by word and deed we might aim to bring others into harmony with Him]… So we are Christ's ambassadors, God making His appeal as it were through us… [Christ's personal representatives]'.*
>
> (2Corinthians 5:19, 21 AMP)

You have a privileged position and responsibility as a royal ambassador, a divine diplomat, a personal representative of God. You are here for such a time as this, called and appointed for God to make His appeal through you.

Have Great Expectations

> **Sing**, O barren one, you who did not bear; break forth into singing and cry aloud, you who did not travail with child! For the [spiritual] children of the desolate one will be more than the children of the married wife, says the Lord.
>
> **Enlarge** the place of your tent, and let the curtains of your habitations be **stretched out; spare not; lengthen** your cords and **strengthen** your stakes, For you will spread abroad to the right hand and to the left; and your offspring will possess the nations and make the desolate cities to be inhabited.
>
> (Isaiah 54:1-3 AMP)

God promises to expand the quality and quantity of your life. So it is time to sing, to enlarge, to stretch out, to spare not, to lengthen and strengthen your restricted thinking that has you expecting lack and not prosperity – that's got you so stuck in barren that you can't imagine bountiful, so that you can receive from God. It is time to take hold of what you do have and allow God to grow it. It is time for your true capacity and potential to be released.

Are you expecting God's favour everywhere you go? Are you expecting God to do wonderful things? Are you expecting Him to make you a blessing to this world?

Jesus often tells me that He's excited about what we're going to do together – which is understandable when you think that they're things long planned – and He wants me to get excited too. I was in the church bookshop a few days after I first heard Him tell me to share His excitement and quite randomly picked out a book. The page I opened on confirmed God's words to me. It said that our attitude should be like Annie's in the song from the musical, always thinking: *'I Love You Tomorrow'*. We should be excited about the future – praying and believing for good things.

You're Wired To Win, Win, Win!

God is a winner. Quite frankly He never ever loses at anything! And He's made us in His image. To win! To succeed. So it's time to expect success.

Most of us would love to do everything well but, in our humanity, we know that we can't. We see Jesus as our role model and we feel even worse. We think: He's perfect and I'm not. We see our flaws and failings. And we allow the breathtaking perfection of Jesus to make us lower our standard. We remember all those times we were told "It's not the winning but the taking part" and settle for making a good effort and hope that'll be OK because God loves us anyway. He does indeed. But we can live better than settling for a good effort.

We get like that because we think of ourselves apart from Jesus. But when we become focused on the fact that His power is within us, we can get excited that He is our standard. When it says in Philippians 4:13 that we can do *all things* that are God's will through Jesus, I don't believe that means just about coping, getting by, scraping in but rather doing them well, that we can actually be GOOD at all those things. We can pray well, wait well, speak well, work well, do well, love well, be a good wife, mother, sister, friend, colleague, lover of Jesus. We can walk this path pre planned by God, enjoying it, exalting Him and doing it well!

We can begin to see the Holy Spirit controlling our words, helping us replace every thought we take captive with truth, leading us in kindness, love, generosity, joy, peace, patience, faith, hope. We can stop expecting failure and start expecting success by God's power. God said to me as I prayed about this year: **"I trust you to do it all well – because you have life in the Spirit."** That was incredibly encouraging. God can have that kind of faith in me, not because I am able, but because He is able and He lives in me!

You can decide you will set out intending to be a winner, to run this race well. You can forget about it not being the winning but taking part. Because it is actually possible to have victory in Jesus every time! I'm not talking about trying to be perfect to earn God's love, and feeling lousy if you mess up, but starting to see just what Jesus can do through and in you instead of holding Him back. You don't have to be intimidated, knocked down and kept down by the devil. You don't have to be manipulated or controlled by him. You can remain stable and be unwilling to give up. You can decide that you're not going to half do life. Instead, **you're really in it to win it.** Staying salty, brightly lit (Matthew 5:13-16), hot, not lukewarm (Revelation 3:16).

Woman of God, you are anointed to run and anointed to win! So rise up and step out empowered to embrace the life you have been given. Stand tall, stand straight, stand strong, stand firm, stand unshakeable. Decide you will live to the max and press on regardless to fulfil your calling, to accomplish God's purpose for your life, that you will overcome the seemingly insurmountable obstacles to flourish and **BECOME** ___Rachael_____ as God wows this world with
(insert your name here)
His beauty, goodness and splendour through His presence living in YOU.

23

Free To Be Wholehearted

In life, before we know it, we can find that we've become very half-hearted women. Outwardly you may seem bubbly, you may work hard at your career, be devoted to your family. But deep down, so much of you has withdrawn from life, and is holding back, so that you can't be hurt or disappointed. But that's not what God wants:

> *"Oh, get up, dear friend,*
> *my fair and beautiful lover – come to me!…*
> ***leave your seclusion,*** *come out in the open.*
> *Let me see your face,*
> *let me hear your voice."*
>
> (Song of Solomon 2 MSG)

God is calling you out of the old shame, out of the hiding and performing to be who you really are. For most of us, this change to be our true selves requires a tremendous shift in our lives that will impact every single area.

Our half-hearted, timid living has come out of so much experience. We've seen that if we let others win and walk all over us then we'll get some peace. They'll be nicer to us, they won't try to manipulate us with their tantrums. They'll ask us to make a choice about something and we'll say we "don't mind" because not asserting any opinions defends us against potential attack and criticism. If you follow your heart, you fear getting opposition.

The fear of failure whispers: "If you give your best and still fail then you truly *are* a failure." "If you wear nice clothes and make an effort but you still look unattractive, then you *are* unattractive." "If you give your best in a relationship and you're still rejected, then that proves you *are* completely undesirable."

There's something in many people that makes them want to look as if their achievements are effortless. We don't want it to seem as if we laboured long and hard, put lots of effort, work or ourselves in. We trick ourselves into believing that really we're great, among the best, if not *the best*, by not putting all we could into things. Then people say: "Wow! She's incredible. If she can do that with no effort, what must she be capable of?!" If we give all we've got then we face that that is as good as it gets and none of us wants to feel that we've exhausted our potential.

Wholehearted Is God's Will For You

But what if you put your whole heart into being yourself? That's God's will for us. Half-hearted living isn't what He has made us for at all.

Half-hearted is not how we are told to seek God:

> *You will find Him if you [truly] seek Him with* **all your heart [and mind] and soul and life.**
> (Deuteronomy 4:29 AMP)

Or love Him:

> *Love the Lord your God with* **all your heart.**
> (Matthew 22:37 NIV)

Or live for Him:

> *Honour the Lord and serve Him* **wholeheartedly.**
> (Joshua 24:14 NLT)

> *Whatever you do, work at it with* **all your heart,** *as working for the Lord, not for men.*
> (Colossians 3:23 NIV)

Wholehearted You Will Prosper

We fear that giving our best and still being found to be lacking writes us off as people.

But nothing can write off the daughters of God. We are complete in Jesus (Colossians 2:10), lacking nothing, and if we would only begin to be our truest selves and rise to our full stature in Him, to stop playing it safe and small, diminishing who we could be, we would find a whole new world opening up. *easier said than done!*

How it must sadden God to see His beautiful daughters living their precious lives anything other than wholeheartedly. God wants us to grow and blossom and flourish, expanding and enlarging, living a life of overflowing abundance and fruitfulness. When you engage your whole heart, stop holding it back in fear and trying to protect it from disappointment, your full creativity and personality have to be put in and used which actually extends the size of your life and dreams. Like that, you will prosper:

> *In everything that he undertook... he sought his God and worked* ***wholeheartedly.*** *And so he* ***prospered.***
> (2Chronicles 31:21 NIV. Referring to Hezekiah.)

Wholehearted Believers

I think that there is a very significant factor that enables a woman to be wholehearted. In fact, I don't believe we can really dare to be wholehearted without it. That is for her to be a BELIEVER. Believers are people of passion. They have a tenacity and stickability that doesn't give up. They've made their choice and will allow nothing to rob it away. Believers actually believe God.

Until a woman really chooses to believe God is who He says He is, He will do what He says He will do and she is who He says she is, fear will continue to assault her and she will listen and walk in it. And fear stops wholeheartedness. Fear makes a woman become half-hearted.

Caleb was a believer. He followed God wholeheartedly – he really believed what God said and that belief was recognised and rewarded. God said: *"But because my servant Caleb has a different spirit and follows me **wholeheartedly**, I will bring him into the land he went to, and his descendants will inherit it"* (Numbers 14:24 NIV).

Caleb believed God's promises. He saw the land of Canaan that God had promised the Israelites they would have as their home. He saw the giants who lived there. But it didn't stop Him believing that the Israelites could take possession. He didn't go along with everybody else (except Joshua) who saw those giants and didn't think God's people stood a chance against them. Caleb spoke from strong conviction. He stayed true to who he was and what he believed. He knew He belonged to a great God. The others just saw a great enemy.

Jesus was also a believer. He was constantly wrongly labelled in His time on earth. But it didn't phase Him. He knew exactly who He was and where He was going. He was totally Himself. He expressed Himself freely and fully in a way that glorified God. He was at ease being Himself. No fear held Him back. Peer pressure didn't pressurise Him. He was different and He didn't care. He was rejected and ridiculed but it didn't stop Him. He was 100% undiluted, 100% uncompromised, 100% Jesus Christ.

AMEN!!!

Jesus had a destiny and nothing could stop Him doing what God had called Him to do. Jesus stuck to His calling and wasn't pushed around. When He began to tell His disciples He was going to be killed (Matthew 16), Peter was horrified. He loved Jesus. He wanted Jesus to stay with them. But Jesus took a stand. He couldn't be swayed by Peter's sympathy. He couldn't let it change God's great purpose for His life – the Salvation of the World.

That's the freedom God wants for us. We're unique. We have a worthwhile and significant purpose. And He desires us to be free to be creative without rules or the fear of judgment.

God has good plans for your life. They really matter. You are able by the Spirit's power. You are born to succeed at everything God has for you to do. So you can put your whole self in to being you and to living your life.

Like Jesus did, we need to know who we are (in God) and where we're going. Your decisions have to be based on what God wants, not what other people want. Jesus calls us to follow Him radically, giving up everything to focus on His way (John 16:24), because He wants us to be wholehearted about God and His plans.

Will You Believe And Go On Believing?

If you are going to **BECOME** _Rachael_____, you need

(insert your name here)

to be a believer. A woman who believes God, about who she is and what He has purposed for her to do, and a woman who **goes on believing God.** As Paul says, we have been transformed from being enemies of God to become His friends but we can't become blasé about it:

> You must **continue to believe** this truth and stand in it firmly. Don't drift away from the assurance you received when you heard the Good News.
>
> (Colossians 1:23 NLT)

Going On Standing In The Truth of Who You Are

The devil doesn't want us to believe God in the first place and he certainly doesn't want us to go on believing Him. We have to recognise his efforts to throw us off course. However free we feel of shame, people can say things to us that can bring out all the old feelings of being rejected, worthless, stupid, disgusting, guilty. We can't let those feelings develop. We have to continue to remember who we are – daughters of the King: loved, adored, protected, full of the Holy Spirit and directed, empowered and helped by Him.

We have to become quick, if people criticise us, not to harbour it and let it become an offence. We can't let it stop us believing we are who God says we are. That doesn't mean we deny our feelings but we take them to God and deny them the right to rule us. If the Holy Spirit convicts you that you've done something wrong, don't let the enemy make you wallow in guilt. Take it to God and pray: "Sorry I sinned, thank you for your forgiveness and that I'm your child and you love me."

Jesus knew who He was, where He had come from and where He was going (John 8:14). He didn't identify with people's opinions of who He was but with God's alone. We need to be so confident of our identity that when people say otherwise, we can say to ourselves: "I don't identify with that. I belong to God."

> 'Remember, no one can make you feel inferior without your consent.'
>
> – Eleanor Roosevelt 1887-1951
> American First Lady

A wholehearted woman is decisive and strong. She breaks out of her shell and becomes the person she is created to be. People can try to push her into their mould but she will consistently be her true self and stick with her calling.

Going On Standing In The Truth Of God's Promises For Your Life

When the devil comes along and tries to tell us that there's no evidence God's promises are true, we have a choice – will we go on believing God? We need to imitate Jesus who always answered lies with God's truth. We need to maintain a wholehearted insistence on what Salvation has achieved for us. Keep Salvation verses to hand – YOUR NEW MIRROR that is in the EXTRAS section at the back of the book. When circumstances fail to line up with the truth of what Jesus has done for you, proclaim that truth.

We need to maintain a wholehearted insistence on God's will. Get hold of those things you know God wants done, and don't have an alternative in view. The devil can try to wear you down when you don't see quick results and tempt you to speak in agreement with him, and not God, by grumbling, talking about the circumstances and your negative feelings. But you can resist him. You can keep your eyes on God and respond by praying, praising and speaking the truth. Every blow you deliver with the sword of the Spirit, that is God's words in the Bible, will weaken his attack. Remember, you are on God's side and God is a winner.

Don't turn the light out on your own future like the spies who went with Caleb to check out the promised land. You can be like them and say: "I've see the bright future God is promising but it's too hard to get it." Or, you can be like Caleb: "I've seen the bright future God is promising and I'm trusting Him to make a way for me to get it."

Daring To Be

'DARE 2 BE'. I saw more than one person wearing clothes with this brand name on them. It took me a while to work out what it said but when I realised the '2' was a number, not the letter 'Z', I could hear God's voice in it. Would I dare to be all He has empowered me to be? Will you dare to put one foot in front of the other as you walk in the Holy Spirit and dare to be all He's empowered **you** to be?

We can't be ashamed of ourselves or of Jesus. For too long people have bought into the false belief that Christianity is ugly, undesirable, embarrassing. Will you stop apologising for being you? You have every right to be your truest self and it's time to stop allowing anyone who would say any different to influence how you feel.

It's time to decide to win, to succeed, to give of your best. Maximum you! Maximum effort! Maximum input! It requires decision, conviction, determination, resolution, passion, consistent belief, the commitment to being all God has made you to be. Amenallujah!

Are you going to be wholehearted about your life, your family, your marriage, your church, your work? Put your heart in? Give 100% your best you? No shame? No embarrassment? Because if you are, I truly believe you will get more out than you have ever dreamt could be possible.

I WANT THIS

24

Free To Enjoy!

Enjoying YOU!

God approves, accepts and enjoys you and you need to approve, accept and ENJOY you too. We've said it over and over again in this book – God is good. All He does is good. He made you and you are a good creation. It's time to actually celebrate being you! You've been considering moving from hiding the things that make you you to accepting them, even letting them shine forth but it's time to go a bit further and actually enjoy them, to be able to say to God: "Thank you that I'm me!".

Take some time now to think about the things that make you you that you've felt ashamed of or hidden, where you've been too guilty or embarrassed to be your real self. Think of the things that you've tried to become that you don't want to be anymore. Think about the lies you've lived, where you've felt guilty for not being/doing what the world wanted or considered best. For example, I decided that I wanted to enjoy my age. I'd always seemed to be either too old or too young but God planned my age and I can enjoy it. I decided to enjoy not being tall. At times I'd worn high heels to compensate but I don't have to – I can actually wear flat shoes and enjoy it and heels when I want to, not because I feel I'm subhuman without them.

Think of the things you admire or value. Christianity is often looked down on and God's values are despised. Faithfulness in marriage, honesty, kindness, not gossiping – so many things that God calls beautiful, the world labels 'unsexy' and 'uncool'. But you can wear God's ways with pride and enjoy the privilege of living a God life.

To get you thinking about enjoying you, fill in some of your top 3's. (Ignore any that are irrelevant to you).

TOP 3 FAVOURITE MEALS
Risotto
Paela
Chicken balti

TOP 3 FAVOURITE GIFTS I WOULD LIKE TO RECEIVE
iPhone
Car
Money

TOP 3 FAVOURITE WAYS TO RELAX
Watching TV/film
Surfing the net
~~Napping~~ Socialising

TOP 3 FAVOURITE SOUNDS
Acoustic guitar
Husky voices
Worshipping people

TOP 3 FAVOURITE SMELLS
Baked bread
Coco Chanel
Fresh washing

TOP 3 FAVOURITE PLACES
Woodstock
Whitcliffe (Ludlow walks)

TOP 3 FAVOURITE THINGS I OWN

TOP 3 PLACES I'D LIKE TO VISIT
Italy
New York

TOP 3 FAVOURITE WEEKEND PLANS

My List Of Things About Being Me That I'm Choosing To Enjoy

My figure
My not-so-delicate ways
My goofiness
Being single
My identity

We live in a world where people compare themselves continuously. We see where we're different from other people and we often wish that we were more like them. But you have been made like you by design. No one else can do what is purposed for you or receive what God has for you. So start to praise God for it. Your gifts may not lie in music, for example, but you don't need to be envious or feel inferior to the great musicians anymore. God is fine with it – it's how He planned you. He's given you other strengths that He wants you to develop.

> *So since we find ourselves fashioned into all these excellently formed and marvellously functioning parts in Christ's body, let's just go ahead and be what we were made to be, without enviously or pridefully comparing ourselves with each other, or trying to be something we aren't.*
>
> (Romans 12:5 MSG)

Shame makes us dwell on our failures but you're freed from that now. Think of some things you do/ have done well. Helped out a friend, learnt to swim, trained your dog, the way you make a great salad… Maybe you didn't get a certificate or praise for it but take some pride in your achievements. Celebrate you and the qualities in you that enable you to do these things.

My List Of Things I've Done/ I Do That I'm Choosing To Celebrate

Grade 5 singing
Making the worship
      team
Being a friend
Making food for
       people

You need to remind yourself that there are no accidents with God. He meant you to be born when you were and to be the age you are now. He's chosen your generation and for you to have a 21st century role. So you can:

BE GLAD FOR ALL GOD'S PLANNING!!!

(Romans 12:12 NLT)

You're in a partnership with the King of Kings and you're God's 'Mrs Right'. You're just RIGHT to be his hands reaching out to those needing His touch. You're just RIGHT to be His feet to go where He leads. You're just RIGHT to be his mouthpiece to reveal His words and will. You're THE ONE He wants to be His helpmate, to accomplish His goals and purpose His dreams with Him. No one else can be the daughter, sister, wife, employee, friend, neighbour, colleague or mother you've been created to be. He wants *you* to love the people in your world with His love because they are just RIGHT to be loved by you.

Begin to be nice to you! Speak well of yourself to yourself. Tell yourself you look nice – not the constant criticism. Tell yourself you're gifted. Say: "I can do it! I can dream with God and achieve those dreams" rather than the condemnation, negativity and doubt. Tell yourself that, by God's power, you can deal with things calmly. Tell yourself that God loves you. He's good to you, has plans to be good to you. He is restoring you and looking after you. Tell yourself that you're excited about life because good things are going to happen to you. This isn't boasting. This isn't pride. This is truth.

Enjoying God!

CELEBRATE GOD ALL DAY, EVERY DAY. I MEAN REVEL IN HIM!
(Philippians 4:4 MSG)

What are all the things that you are coming to love about God, Jesus and the Holy Spirit? Tell them as you make a list to end this Psalm:

> My heart overflows with a beautiful thought!
> I will recite a lovely poem to the King,
> For my tongue is like the pen of a skilful poet.
> You are the most handsome of all.
> Gracious words stream from your lips…

(Psalm 45:1-2 NLT)

Endless mercy ⓑ
Mighty love
Best friend
Abba Father
The Way

Refuge
Safe place

Enjoying Living!

I realised one day that I was actually living my dream. I had the 'real deal' – I was happy and fulfilled loving God. Always receiving new revelation, I could never become bored of the adventure of knowing God. I was even doing His will – living in His vision for my life. The thing was that I wasn't enjoying it. Not because it wasn't totally enjoyable, but because for so long I had searched for truth, searched for fulfilment, I was in shock. **The search was over!** I needed to relax so that I could begin to enjoy it.

How about you? Do you need to start to take pleasure in God and the life

He has given to you. You have your happily ever after. You have your Prince – Jesus. You have the royal lifestyle. No more Cinderella. You have been transformed into a beautiful Princess. FOREVER.

Clearing The Way

Back in Chapter 8, I suggested throwing away anything with an unflattering nickname on. But there may be even more than that you would like to be rid of. Do you have things you've inherited, gifts you've been given or clothes in your wardrobe that you don't like, that just aren't 'you'? Do you have school reports, sentimental memorabilia from old relationships, photographs etc. that bring back bad memories/ hold a part of you emotionally in the past/ are negative about your identity/ speak of the person you no longer want to be?

Perhaps you've got some lucky symbols like birthstones, horseshoes, figures of saints, zodiac charms, something with another religion's blessing inscribed on it, or any gods like statues of Buddha. Or you may have books or music with subject matter that is offensive to God.

This is an opportunity to go round your house with Jesus and ask Him to show you things that aren't about a life of companionship and participation with Him. Ask Him what you should do with anything He wants you to get rid of – should you destroy it or can your cast-offs bless someone else? Don't allow the devil to make you feel guilty about doing what Jesus says. You wouldn't want someone to keep something you'd given, or left, to them if it was compromising them *BECOMING* _____.
(insert THEIR name here)
Nor would they want it for you…

Your home can be a place that speaks of who you truly are – a place full of the beauty of God.

If You Take One Thing...

If I could get you to take just one thing from this part of the book, it is:

Don't settle for half.

I don't want you to:

- Only half become all you could be.
- Only half allow yourself to dream.
- Only get half a vision for your life.
- Limit yourself to only half relying on Jesus' ability within you.
- Live halfway between failure and success.
- Be half-hearted and only half believe God.
- Only half enjoy everything.

Don't allow ANYTHING to stop you receiving God's best.

YOU are the woman God is with!

And…

WITH GOD <u>ALL THINGS</u> ARE POSSIBLE.
(Matthew 19:16 NIV)

AFTER

25

The Woman You See NOW

This book's part in your journey to **BECOMING** _Rachael_
(insert your name here)
is nearly over. But the real book – the eternal story of you being yourself is
beginning. Do you remember the assessment you did of yourself at the
start? Do you remember who the woman was you saw when you looked at
yourself – all the things that you needed to improve, all the times you'd
failed? What about the woman you see now?

She Knows Who She Is

The woman you see now should feel that she has a far greater idea who she
is and is beginning to like and appreciate it. She is **BECOMING**
Rachael, and she doesn't want to be anyone else. She
(insert your name here)
has a 100% devotion to God and doing life with Him, His way, that is 100%
non negotiable. She has such a strong sense of her identity in Him that
when people attack it, it doesn't make a ripple.

When she looks in the mirror, she sees a body that she is learning to love
and look after because it is home to the Spirit of God. God has bestowed
His glory upon her and she calls herself: "Beautiful."

She Knows Whose She Is

The real you knows that she belongs to God, made for companionship and
participation with Jesus. She knows that she is loved. And she knows that
nothing can match God. He is the 'real deal' and there is always more to
inspire awe and wonder in her.

She Knows What Is Hers

The real you knows that she's got Salvation. That's provision for absolutely everything. She has royal status. She shares Jesus' throne and reigns with Him.

She Knows Where She Is Going

The real you may not know exactly what God's great plans for her life are yet but she knows that He is going to tell her in His perfect timing, that He's not holding out on her. She's ready with a smile for that future that He's preparing. She's looking to Him for the necessary strategy to get her where He wants her to be. And she's looking to His Spirit, in her, to empower her all the way to Eternity. Yes! She knows at the end of the day that she belongs in Heaven and that's where she'll spend forever when her time on Earth is done. In the meantime, she has conviction about the life she wants to live for God that's strong enough to stop her allowing herself to be pushed around.

She Knows Who Others Are

The real you has received God's love so she can love people just for being them and regard them as equals who share her value because they too are created by God.

Yourself and You

Remember the first exercise you did, right the way back at the beginning of Chapter 1? Well, close your eyes and imagine that scenario again. This time, see the real you standing in that room of glamorous strangers. How do you look? What are you doing?

~~tn to~~ I am at Soul Survivor worshipping Jesus. I look radiant.

What do your eyes look like? Bright, shining, full of light?

Looking to Jesus - in love, hopeful, secure, loved.

What's the expression on your face? Relaxed, smiling, laughing?

Smiling and relaxed. I'm singing.

What are you wearing? Clothes you feel comfortable in that reflect your own taste and style?

Yes. A white top and shorts. I think I have a hairband in too... Totally just the clothes that express me.

What's your posture like? Confident, free, alive?

Stretched up, hands in the air worshipping, confident, alive, free, tall, strong.

Do you see that the tense, withdrawn, uncertain, afraid or loud mouthed, dominating woman you saw before, who was hiding in various ways, is now a woman who is accompanied by Jesus? She is full of His Spirit and has Him by her side to guide and support her. When He walked on the earth, there was something about His presence. Something irresistible. Huge crowds literally chased after Him. He's the One she's with. And she is full of the glory of God – warm, confident, relaxed, at ease, radiant, happy, fulfilled, present, engaging with people, kind, deeply respectful, loving, wholehearted, calm, peaceful, content, successful.

Enjoy looking at the real you and feeling what it's like to see, hear and feel through her. This is who you really are!

Think of her in different places with different people. What are your feelings towards her now? Don't you find you like her where before you felt harsh towards her, were looking down on her? That you're rooting for her now, you're behind her all the way, you want her to fulfill her potential?

Who is the woman you see now? God's lovely creation, exquisitely made, partnering with the King. What an opposite to that girl whose *glory* was *in her shame* (Philippians 3:18-19 NIV). Her value doesn't come from any of the old things it used to like how she looks, her talents, education, partner, children, friends or church. Instead she finds her worth, place and confidence in Jesus alone. She has a single aim: that every facet of her life and self should scream the reality of her amazing God.

> *We don't go around preaching about ourselves; we preach Christ Jesus, the Lord. All we say about ourselves is that we are your servant because of what Jesus has done for us. For God, who said, "Let there be light in the darkness," has made us understand that this light is the brightness of the glory of God that is seen in the face of Jesus Christ.*
>
> *But this precious treasure — this light and power that now shine within us — is held in perishable containers, that is, in our weak bodies. So everyone can see that* **our glorious power is from God and is not our own.**
>
> (2 Corinthians 4:5-7, 15 NLT)

And God created you. Made to...

BE Rachael

(insert your name here)

SO:

Arise! [from the depression and prostration in which circumstances have kept you – **rise to a new life]!** *Shine (be radiant with the glory of the Lord), for your light has come, and the glory of the Lord has risen upon you!*

And nations shall come to your light, and kings to the brightness of your rising.

(Isaiah 60:1, 3 AMP)

EXTRAS

Your New Mirror

The woman the mirror reflects:

IS FORGIVEN
*He is so rich in kindness that he purchased **insert your name here** freedom through the blood of his Son, and **her** sins are FORGIVEN. He has showered His kindness on **her**, along with all wisdom and understanding.*

(Ephesians 1:7-8 NLT)

IS RIGHT WITH GOD
*God made Christ, who never sinned, to be the offering for **insert your name here** sin, so that **she** could be made RIGHT WITH GOD through Christ.*

(2Corinthians 5:21 NLT)

IS WHOLE
*He has borne **insert your name here** griefs (sicknesses, weaknesses, and distresses) and carried **her** sorrows and pains [of punishment]… He was wounded for **her** transgressions, He was bruised for **her** guilt and iniquities; the chastisement [needful to obtain] peace and well-being was upon Him, and with the stripes [that wounded] Him **she** is HEALED AND MADE WHOLE.*

(Isaiah 53:4-5 AMP)

HAS A GREAT LIFE TO LIVE
*I came that **insert your name here** may have and enjoy life, and have it in abundance (to the full, till it overflows).*

(John 10:10 AMP)

IS GOING TO LIVE FOREVER
***Insert your name here** has been born again. **Her** new life did not come from her earthly parents because the life they gave **her** will end in death. But this new life will last forever because it comes from the eternal, living word of God.*

(1Peter 1:23 NLT)

HAS BEEN RESCUED FROM THE DEVIL'S RULE

*He has rescued **insert your name here** from the one who rules in the kingdom of darkness, and He has brought **her** into the Kingdom of His dear son.*

(Colossians 1:13 NLT)

IS BLESSED (HAPPY, FORTUNATE AND TO BE ENVIED) (AMP)

*Through the work of Christ Jesus, God has blessed **insert your name here** with the same blessing He promised to Abraham.*

(Galatians 3:14 NLT)

*Blessed shall **insert your name here** be in the city and blessed shall **she** be in the field.*
*Blessed shall be the fruit of **her** body and the fruit of **her** ground…*
*Blessed shall be **her** basket and **her** kneading trough.*
*Blessed shall **she** be when she comes in and blessed shall **she** be when **she** goes out.*
*The Lord shall cause **her** enemies who rise up against **her** to be defeated before **her** face; they shall come out against **her** one way and flee before **her** seven ways.*
*The Lord shall command the blessing upon **her** in her storehouse and in all that **she** undertakes. And He shall bless **her** in the land which the Lord **her** God gives **her**…*
*And the Lord shall make **her** have a surplus of prosperity, through the fruit of **her** body, of **her** livestock, and of **her** ground…*
*The Lord shall open to **her** His good treasury, the heavens, to give the rain of **her** land in its season and to bless all the work of **her** hands; and **she** shall lend to many nations, but **she** shall not borrow.*
*And the Lord shall make **her** the head, and not the tail; and **she** shall be above only, and **she** shall not be beneath.*

(Deuteronomy 28:1-13 AMP)

HAS GREAT WEALTH

*Though He [Christ] was very rich, yet for **insert your name here** sake He became poor, so that by His poverty He could make **her** rich.*

(2Corinthians 8:9 NLT)

CAN BOLDLY APPROACH GOD

Insert your name here *can boldly enter heaven's Most Holy Place because of the blood of Jesus.*

(Hebrews 10:19 NLT)

Hallelujah.

IS FREE FROM THE POWER OF SIN

***Insert your name here** old sinful self was crucified with Christ so that sin might lose its power in **her** life. **She** is no longer slave to sin. For when **she** died with Christ **she** was set free from the power of sin. And since **she** died with Christ, **she** knows **she** will also share His new life. **She** is sure of this because Christ rose from the dead, and He will never die again. Death no longer has any power over Him. He died once to defeat sin, and now He lives for the glory of God. So **she** should consider herself dead to sin and able to live for the glory of God through Christ Jesus.*

(Romans 6:6-11 NLT)

IS FREE FROM ANY CONDEMNATION

*If God is for **insert your name here**, who can ever be against **her**? Since God did not spare even His own Son but gave Him up for **her**, won't God, who gave **her** Christ, also give **her** everything else? Who dares accuse **her** whom God has chosen for His own? Will God? No! He is the one who has given **her** right standing with Himself. Who then will condemn her? Will Christ Jesus? No, for He is the one who died for **her** and was raised to life for **her** and is sitting at the place of highest honour next to God, pleading for **her**.*

(Romans 8:31-35 NLT)

HAS BEEN GIVEN AUTHORITY

***Insert your name here** has been given the keys of the kingdom of heaven; and whatever **she** binds (declares to be improper and unlawful) on earth must be what is already bound in heaven; and whatever **she** looses (declares lawful) on earth must be what is already loosed in heaven.*

(Matthew 16:19 AMP)

God gave Adam and Eve authority and dominion and He has restored it to you that you might rule and reign on this earth, binding the work of the devil and releasing the purposes of God in Jesus' name.

IS ROYALTY

***Insert your name here** is a member of a chosen people, a royal priesthood, a holy nation, His own special person, that **she** may proclaim the praises of Him who called **her** out of darkness into His marvellous light.*

(1Peter 2:9 NKJV)

IS FEARLESS
For God has not given **insert your name here** *a spirit of fear but of power and of love and of a sound mind.*
(2Timothy 1:7 NKJV)

IS CAPABLE
Insert your name here *can do all things through Christ who strengthens **her**.*
(Philippians 4:13 NKJV)

ETC. ETC. ETC.
This is just a glimpse of what the Bible has to say about your true identity.[lxvi]

Kisses for You

HIS WORDS ARE KISSES, HIS KISSES WORDS

(Song of Solomon 4, MSG)

Here are some of those kisses for you to cut out and stick on the mirror, by your bed, in the car – wherever. There are some gaps for you to write your own – when God kisses you, write it down and carry it with you.[67]

I have strength for all things in Christ who empowers me [I am ready for anything and equal to anything through Him who infuses inner strength into me; I am self-sufficient in Christ's sufficiency]. (Philippians 4:13 AMP)	The Lord is my Helper, and I am not afraid of anything that mere man can do to me. (Hebrews 13:6 TLB)
I love God truly [with affectionate reverence, prompt obedience, and grateful recognition of His blessing], I am known by God [recognized as worthy of His intimacy and love, and I am owned by Him]. (1 Corinthians 8:3 AMP)	My body is the temple (the very sanctuary) of the Holy Spirit who lives within me, whom I have received [as a Gift] from God. I am not my own, I was bought with a price [purchased with a preciousness and paid for, made His own]. (1 Corinthians 6:19-20 AMP)
God has plans of peace… of prosperity… to give me a future and a hope. (Jeremiah 29:11 NKJV)	My God will liberally supply (fill to the full) my every need according to His riches in glory in Christ Jesus. (Philippians 4:19 AMP)
I seek my happiness in the Lord, and he gives me my heart's desire. I give myself to the Lord; trust in him, and he helps me; he makes my righteousness shine like the noonday sun. (Psalm 37:4-6 GNB)	I walk in love, [esteeming and delighting in others] as Christ loved me and gave himself up for me, a slain offering and sacrifice to God [for me, so that it became] a sweet fragrance. (Ephesians 5:2 AMP)

I carefully build myself up in this most holy faith by praying in the Holy Spirit, staying right at the centre of God's love, keeping my arms open and outstretched, ready for the mercy of my Master, Jesus Christ. This is the unending life, the real life! (Jude 20-21 MSG)	God has chosen me. He will strengthen me. He will help me. He will uphold me with His victorious right hand. (Isaiah 41 NLT)
God has good thoughts and plans toward me. He intends for me to have peace and not evil and to give me hope in my final outcome. (Jeremiah 29:11 AMP)	I am my lover's. I'm all He wants. I'm all the world to Him. (Song of Solomon 7 MSG)
God has chosen me. (John 15:16 AMP)	He will lift me up and make my life significant. (James 4:10 AMP)
When I go someplace and the people don't receive and accept me, I don't let it get me down, I just shake it off and go on about my business. (Luke 10:10-11 AMP)	I am clothed with the beauty that comes from within – the unfading beauty of a gentle and quiet spirit, which is so precious to God. (1 Peter 3:4 NLT)
I am beautiful. My beauty is perfect. (Song of Solomon 4 NLT, Ezekiel 16 NIV)	I have run to God and run from evil. My body will glow with health, my very bones will vibrate with life! (Proverbs 3:7-8 MSG)
I am created anew in Christ Jesus, so that I can do the good things He planned for me long ago. (Ephesians 2:10 NLT)	I trust in the Lord with all my heart, and do not lean on my own understanding; in all my ways I acknowledge Him and He directs my paths. (Proverbs 3:5-6 NKJV)
God ♥ me. (Isaiah 43:44 NLT)	God delights in me. (Psalm 149:4 NLT)
I am assured and know that [God being a partner in my labour] all things work together and are [fitting into a plan] for good to and for me who loves God and is called according to [His] design and purpose. (Romans 8:28 AMP)	I am God's MASTERPIECE. (Ephesians 2: 0 NLT)

Notes

CHAPTER 2

1   *Daily Telegraph* 11/4/06

2   Top Sante magazine's survey, quoted in *Daily Telegraph* 2/8/05

3   Michelle Graham, *Wanting To Be Her.* InterVarsity Press, 2005.

4   *Vogue* magazine, January 2006

CHAPTER 3

5   (Isaiah 45:5 AMP)

6   (Psalm 136:6 AMP)

7   (Ephesians 1:4 MSG)

8   (Psalm 139:13 AMP)

9   (Psalm 139:14 NIV)

10   (Genesis 1:27 NLT)

11   (Psalm 71:6 NIV)

12   (Psalm 139:1 NLT)

13   (Psalm 139:2 NLT)

14   (Psalm 139:3 NIV)

15   (Psalm 139:3 NLT)

16   (Psalm 139:4 NLT)

17   (Psalm 139:17-18 NLT)

18   (Jeremiah 29:11 NKJV)

19   (Psalm 45:11 NIV)

20   (John 3:16-17 NLT)

21   (John 10:10 AMP)

22   (2Corinthians 5:18 NLT)

23   (John 1:12-13 NLT)

24   (Ephesians 2:10 AMP)

25   (Jeremiah 29:11 NIV)

26   (Isaiah 61:7 NLT)

27   (Romans 3:8-9 NLT)

28   (Psalm 121:7 NIV)

29   (Psalm 68:19 NLT)

30   (Psalm 23:6 NAS)

31   (Jeremiah 33:3 NIV)

32   (Ephesians 3:30 MSG)

33   Some of these verses have been put into the first person voice of God.

CHAPTER 6

34 Reprinted by permission. Juan Carlos Ortiz, *Living With Jesus Today*. Triangle, SPCK, 1982.

CHAPTER 8

35 Derek Prince, *Blessing or Curse*. Chosen Books, 1990.

CHAPTER 9

36 Trinny Woodall and Susannah Constantine, *What You Wear Can Change Your Life*. Weidenfeld and Nicolson, 2004.

37 *Vogue* magazine, December 2005

38 *Vogue* magazine, December 2005

CHAPTER 11

39 Michelle McKinney Hammond, *A Sassy Girl's Guide to Loving God*. Harvest House, 2002.

40 John and Stasi Eldredge, *Captivating*, 2005, Thomas Nelson Inc. Nashville, Tennessee. All rights reserved.

41 Joyce Meyer, 'True Love You Are The Apple of God's Eye', feature article, *Enjoying Everyday Life* magazine, February 2007.

42 Angela Thomas, *My Single Mom Life*. Thomas Nelson, 2007.

CHAPTER 12

43 Plum Sykes, *Bergdorf Blondes*. Penguin Books, 2004.

44 Darlene Zschech, *The Kiss of Heaven*. Bethany House, 2003.

45 C.S. Lewis, *Weight of Glory: And Other Addresses*. Harper Collins, 2001.

CHAPTER 13

46 Nigel Hemming, 1998, ©Vineyard Songs.

CHAPTER 14

47 *The Stepford Wives* is a 1972 novel by Ira Levin and films (1975 and 2004) about women who are gynoids (female robots) programmed to be fawning, submissive and impossibly beautiful housewives.

48 The Pharisees were a Jewish religious group that zealously followed the Old Testament laws and their own religious traditions.

49 The father celebrates the return and repentance of his prodigal younger son which the elder brother feels is unfair: "All these years I've worked hard for you and never once refused to do a single thing you told me to. And in all that time you never gave me even one young goat for a feast with my friends" (Luke 16:29 NLT).

CHAPTER 15

50 Sylvia Mary Alison, *God is Building A House*. John Hunt, 2002.

51   Brother Lawrence, Translated by E.M. Blaiklock, *The Practice of the Presence of God.* Hodder and Stoughton, 1981.

52   Jesse Duplantis, *Voice of the Covenant* magazine, February 2006.

53   From Bill Hybels' sermon at HTB on 14 May 2006. The full sermon can be downloaded free at www.htb.org.uk.

54   Reprinted by permission. Juan Carlos Ortiz, *Living With Jesus Everyday.* Triangle, SPCK, 1982.

55   Jackie Pullinger, *Chasing The Dragon.* Hodder and Stoughton, 1980.

CHAPTER 16

56   Dom Vitalis Lehodey, *Quoted Contemplative Prayer.* Ligouri Publications, 1979.

57   Joyce Huggett, *Listening to God: Hearing His Voice.* Hodder and Stoughton, 1986.

58   Reprinted by permission. Rebecca, quoted in *Christianity* magazine, July 2005.

59   Reprinted by permission. Anne Hibbert, quoted in *Christianity* magazine, July 2005.

60   Derek Prince, *Thanksgiving, Praise and Worship.* DPM, 1990.

61   John Eldredge, *The Journey of Desire.* Thomas Nelson, 2000.

62   Reprinted by permission. Bobbie Houston, *Heaven Is In This House.* Maximised Leadership Incorporated, 2001.

CHAPTER 17

63   Agnes Sanford, *Creation Waits,* Logos International.

CHAPTER 19

64   First three questions quoted from Mike Murdoch.

CHAPTER 21

65   James Friesen, *The Life Model: Living From The Heart Jesus Gave You.* Shepherds House Inc., 1999.

YOUR NEW MIRROR

66   These verses have been put into the 3rd person feminine singular.

KISSES FOR YOU

67   These verses have been put into the first person.

Eternally Grateful

This book was God's idea, born out of my own experience of becoming me which owes everything to Him.

I am so grateful to God for all the people and resources He has brought into my life, and placed in my hands, often in extraordinary ways, and always at exactly the right moment.

Some are quoted in this book and I know you will want to join me in thanking the authors.

I would particularly like to publicly honour the following:

My Father (d.2002) – For living life in a way that revealed the reality of God and made me determined to find what he had and what made him the way I wanted to be.

My Mother – For never failing to find love, encouragement, inspiration and ideas for me in all my stages of becoming. No words can express my love and thanks.

My sister, Sophie (d.1998) – For bringing so much fun into my life and encouraging me to make a start with Isla and a purple notebook.

My sister, Victoria – For being the most amazing, supportive, fun and creative person who constantly brings wisdom and blessing into my life.

My grandparents and uncle, Michael – For continuing to take an interest and believe in me – it has meant a lot.

All leadership at HTB, 2002-2005, especially:

Deirdre Hurst – For prayer meetings. You made a difference to my life!

Michael Alison – For living a faith that made him stand out of the crowd.

Jez Barnes – For a life-changing sermon, 20 June 2004.

James, George, Emi-Lou and all participants – For pastorate and homegroup.

All leadership at Herts International Church – for making a place where miracles *do* happen. Especially:

Brad Norman – For always speaking God's words into my life and being a role

model of what can be achieved when somebody steps up to their calling.
Peter Bellingan – For changing my life by explaining 'faith'.

For bringing truth and encouragement into my life with their books/ talks/
resources:
Mike Bickle, Jesse and Cathy Duplantis, John Eldredge, Bobbie Houston, Joyce
Huggett, Bill Johnson, Lance Lambert, Terry Law, Joyce Meyer, Derek Prince,
Agnes Sanford, Angela Thomas, Steve and Jenny Watson.

Charlotte – For photography.

Jeremy and team – For all their work in preparing the book for publication.

ANNA SYMONDS

Anna has a background in History of Art, has worked with historic costume at the museum at Kensington Palace, run style workshops and been involved in helping women with their body image issues.

The highs and lows of her own life, her search for purpose and the resulting pursuit of God, form the basis of this book.

She offers individual support, and runs group workshops, for women.

She would love to hear your experiences of Becoming You and can be contacted through the website.

BECOMING AND BEING YOU

- Individual support

- Small group workshops

- BUY THE BOOK!

www.annasymonds.com